Poetry of the Law

Poetry of the Law

From Chaucer to the Present

Edited by David Kader
and Michael Stanford

UNIVERSITY OF IOWA PRESS
IOWA CITY

University of Iowa Press, Iowa City 52242

www.uiowapress.org
Printed in the United States of America

Design by Ashley Muehlbauer

The University of Iowa Press is a member of Green Press Initiative and is committed to preserving natural resources.

Printed on acid-free paper

Library of Congress Cataloging-in-Publication Data
Poetry of the law: from Chaucer to the present / edited by David Kader and Michael Stanford.
p. cm.
Includes index.
ISBN-13: 978-1-58729-866-0 (pbk.)
ISBN-10: 1-58729-866-X (pbk.)
1. English poetry. 2. American poetry. 3. Law—Poetry. 4. Lawyers—Poetry. 5. Judges—Poetry. 6. Trials—Poetry. 7. Punishment—Poetry. I. Kader, David, 1947– II. Stanford, Michael (Michael Kent)
PR1195.L37P64 2010
821.008'0352344—dc22 2009030983

In memory of our parents,

Israel Moshe Kader and Lola Kader,

Colonel Norman Stanford and Patricia Wallace Stanford

The oldest hath borne most; we that are young
Shall never see so much, nor live so long.
KING LEAR, 5.3.326–7.

Contents

Acknowledgments

We owe a great debt to our former dean, Patricia White, whose generous support of our work on this anthology was indispensable. Rebecca Tanghe's extraordinary secretarial contribution to a myriad of technical aspects of the project was always superb. Our gratitude is substantial, as well, to many others on the staff of our law school, including Christopher Baier, Mary Lemon, Nanci Beardsley, Jenny Bishop, Judy Karls, Marianne Alcorn, and Elizabeth DiFelice. We are indebted to the staffs of the libraries at Arizona State University—the Hayden Library and the John J. Ross and William C. Blakely Law Library. For unfailing encouragement through the long gestation of this project and for expert editorial support, we are pleased to acknowledge Joseph Parsons of the University of Iowa Press. We are also grateful for the unflagging support of many at the University of Iowa Press, especially Charlotte Wright for her expert management of the book's editorial stage and Rebecca Marsh for her superb copy editing of the manuscript.

During his work on this book, Michael Stanford received invaluable advice and support from literary, legal, and scholarly friends, particularly his colleagues at the Barrett Honors College (the best of teachers) and the Maricopa County Public Defender's Office (the best of lawyers). His special thanks go to Karen Bruhn, Karin Horwatt Cather, Stephanie Conlon, Noel Fidel, Kathleen Heil, Jeff Kirchler, David Pickus, Jennifer Roach, Jacquie Scott, Jerald Schreck, and Fredrica Strumpf. And obviously, as always, to Lindy Stanford.

During his work on this book, David Kader received much aid and comfort from library staffs nearly coast-to-coast and across the Atlantic and Pacific, where he was teaching and researching: the H. Douglas Barclay Law Library of Syracuse University, the Library of the Institute of Advanced Legal Studies in London, England, and Wuhan University Library in Wuhan, P.R. China. His special thanks go to Michael Loring, Ritta Halperin, Patricia A. Schneider, Philip Levine, Chuck Hanzlicek, John M. Junker, Robert F. Utter, Avrom Sherr, and Bop. Much love to Charnya and Fishel, and to Aaron M. and Jamie S. and their beloved Ezra, and to Sarah E.; and all my heart to Pattie.

Introduction

This is the first anthology of poetry about the law to be published in the United States in half a century and the first *selective* anthology on the subject ever published.[1] It includes the work of many of the most distinguished English-language poets in the six centuries from Chaucer to the present. We thus aim to fill a striking gap in the universe of contemporary poetry anthologies, which includes, after all, multiple collections of poems focused on such central human concerns as love, war, and politics, as well as anthologies devoted to more specialized topics like travel, sports, dogs, cats, birds, flowers, mothers, fathers, and poetry itself. A subject as interesting and consequential as the law would seem to merit at least a single anthology. The abiding popularity of law-related films and novels makes it even more surprising that no one has yet made a serious attempt to gather the poetry of the law.

A parallel gap appears in the realm of literary scholarship. In 1973, James Boyd White's *The Legal Imagination*[2] inaugurated the scholarly study of law and literature. Since then, it has burgeoned as an academic field, yielding dozens of books, hundreds of articles, and several specialized journals. Yet for all the richness of this scholarship, it has focused almost entirely on fiction and drama.[3] In the third edition of his survey *Law and Literature*, Judge Richard Posner reduces the subject of law-related poetry, literally, to a footnote, which declares, "Relatively few short poems take law as their theme."[4]

If Posner is correct, we might ask why this should be so. It may be that law—as either profession or subject matter—is fundamentally incompatible with poetry. This was the view expressed by William Blackstone, the great eighteenth-century legal scholar and author of the *Commentaries on the Laws of England*. In 1741, at the age of eighteen, Blackstone enrolled in the Middle Temple to study law. For the previous three years, he had been at Oxford, where he had devoted himself to reading and writing poetry. About the time he entered the Middle Temple, he wrote a remarkable and little-known poem, "The Lawyer's Farewell to His Muse."

Blackstone complains that while his "tender age" had been spent in the "shady grove[s]" and "warbling . . . woods" of poetry, he now finds himself exiled to a grimly adult place, the metropolis of law: “Me wrangling courts, and stubborn law, / To smoke, and crowds, and cities draw: / There selfish faction rules the day, / And pride and avarice throng the way.” Blackstone contrasts the grimy world of the law, with its attention to every form of human conflict, to the pure and “blithsome” world of poetry. One might think that the turbulence of social reality would provide at least a certain excitement lacking in the poet’s warbling woods. Unfortunately, the law turns out to be as tedious in its operations as it is sordid in its concerns: “a formal band / In furs, and coifs around me stand; / With sounds uncouth and accents dry, / That grate the soul of harmony.” In the phrase “sounds uncouth,” Blackstone rehearses a traditional point about the supposed ugliness of legal language.

Yet the poem’s conclusion shows Blackstone facing his new life with stoicism, hopeful that if he can penetrate beyond “the bulwarks of the law,” he will encounter “justice” itself—figured as a female divinity who is specifically not a muse, a “venerable maid” in contrast to the “celestial nymph” of poetry. Thus, Blackstone’s “Farewell” draws a complete, schematic opposition between poetry and the law. Poetry is celestial, pastoral, solitary, and mellifluous; law is venerable, social, urban, and cacophonous. Blackstone’s antitheses, however, are rooted in a particularly Augustan sense of literary decorum, one not always shared by writers of other periods. During the Elizabethan era, for example, London’s law schools, the Inns of Court, constituted as much a literary milieu as a legal one. The young aristocrats who enrolled there competed enthusiastically in the production of poetry, much of it employing legal images. John Donne, who studied at Lincoln’s Inn although he was never called to the bar, devotes his second satire to ridiculing the fictional Coscus, a bad poet who becomes a worse lawyer. Yet, early and late, Donne’s own poetry makes elegant, judicious use of the concepts and language of the common law. So do the sonnets of Shakespeare, who had many connections with the Inns. Presumably not even Blackstone could deny the beauty of Sonnet 30’s opening lines: “When to the sessions of sweet silent thought / I summon up remembrance of things past.” Yet this passage loses much of its meaning if we miss the metaphor of memory as a court in session, issuing summonses for vanished things and people to appear.

In Blackstone’s own century, Alexander Pope and Jonathan Swift find law a fertile subject for poetic satire. In the Victorian period, Robert Browning bases his masterpiece, the long narrative poem *The Ring and the Book,* on the true story of a murder and its legal aftermath, offering numerous reflections on the law along the way. Browning's great American contemporaries, Walt Whitman and Emily Dickinson, make frequent use of legal settings and images. It is the twentieth and twenty-first centuries, however, that have seen the greatest density of law-related poems. The post-Victorian broadening of poetry's subject matter has meant that more and more modern poets have chosen to write poems centered on the law. Some of these poets—Edgar Lee Masters, Charles Reznikoff, Roy Fuller, Brad Leithauser, Lawrence Joseph, Martín Espada, Seth Abramson—have themselves been lawyers or, at least, law-trained. Reznikoff is an especially interesting example because—in complete contradiction to Blackstone—he gives his legal education credit for forming his aesthetic as a poet. A larger group, including some of the most distinguished of modern poets, peers (or squints) at the legal system from outside. Thus, we would differ from Posner enough to say that, while law-focused poems have indeed been rarer than law-focused novels or plays, they have been plentiful enough, especially in the past century, to warrant at least an anthology of their own.

A search through the stacks of several university libraries (augmented by online research and the suggestions of poets and lawyers) yielded some two hundred compelling law-related poems, from which the present selection of an even hundred has been made. By "law-related poem" we mean a poem with a legal setting (the courtroom, the lawyer's office, the judge's chambers, the law-school classroom) or a poem largely organized around legal issues, concepts, metaphors, or language. We have included a few excerpts from long narrative poems (*The Canterbury Tales, Don Juan, The Ring and the Book, John Brown's Body*), though for the most part we present complete short poems—lyrics, satires, and dramatic monologues.[5]

The poems sort themselves into roughly six overlapping categories.

POEMS ABOUT LAWYERS AND JUDGES

Chaucer gives us the first significant portrait of a lawyer in English poetry. His Sergeant of the Law comes across as a distinctly mixed figure—learned, industrious, and skillful, if also self-important and a little too interested in enriching himself. Four centuries later George Crabbe offers a similarly shaded portrait of a lawyer who, although rendered cynical by experience, nevertheless deals humanely and conscientiously with his clients.

For the most part, though, poems about lawyers tend to divide into what we call Good Lawyer and Bad Lawyer poems. Thus, John Donne blasts "Coscus" for his greed and corruption, declaring acidly: "men which choose / Law practice for mere gain, . . . repute / Worse than imbrothel'd strumpets prostitute." Meanwhile Donne's contemporary Ben Jonson writes a poem extolling the ideal lawyer, who never presses a case without merit and who engages in litigation only as a last resort—but who, once forced into court, becomes a ferocious warrior in his client's behalf. In the eighteenth century, Jonathan Swift produces a Good Lawyer poem with a twist, ridiculing lawyers in general by way of praising his friend Robert Lindsay as the exception that proves the rule. Swift's "Answer to 'Paulus'" reads like a high-spirited poetic footnote to the famous blast at lawyers in *Gulliver's Travels*. In the twentieth century, Carl Sandburg ("The Lawyers Know Too Much") gives a populist American twist to the Bad Lawyer poem, condemning lawyers as both "slippery" in their manipulation of language and innately reactionary in their reliance on tradition (they "know / a dead man's thoughts too well"). Meanwhile a very different poet, Yvor Winters, in his eulogy of the defense attorney Edwin McKenzie, offers an opposite but equally American conception of the lawyer as a lonely, embattled champion of individual rights.

A smaller subset of poems deals with judges, rarely in positive terms. Percy Bysshe Shelley mounts a savage if understandable ad hominem attack on the Lord Chancellor who issued a decree depriving Shelley of custody of his children after his wife's suicide. In his "Judge Selah Lively," Edgar Lee Masters gives a trial attorney's jaundiced portrait of a fictional judge who is, in every sense, a small man. Meanwhile, D. H. Lawrence expresses the artist's perennial indignation at censorship when he mocks the octogenarian magistrate who ordered thirteen of Lawrence's paintings seized as obscene. In his quirky poem "The Law Has Reasons," David Ignatow offers a somewhat less negative view of judges, depicting them as ghostly and rather pitiable figures, sitting in well-dusted chambers listening for the "exact word" of the law.

POEMS ABOUT THE CITIZEN IN THE LEGAL SYSTEM

In "The Witness," Ted Kooser depicts a woman waiting, in an attitude of tense resignation, to be called to the stand as a witness in a divorce action. In "Twelve Chairs," Rita Dove imagines the twelve distinct psychologies that a panel of jurors might bring to its task. Kooser and Dove present what seem to be neutral perspectives on the law. For the most part, though, when poets write about nonlawyers enmeshed in the legal system, it is with a sense of the harshness of the system toward the people caught in its toils. The legal aid lawyer in Martín Espada's "Mi Vida: Wings of Fright" cannot save his immigrant clients from being evicted by their landlords, let alone cure the multiple traumas they have experienced on their desperate journeys to the U.S. In "'Butch' Weldy," Edgar Lee Masters depicts a workman blinded in an industrial accident, pathetically bewildered by the callous "fellow-servant" doctrine that will prevent him from recovering for his injuries.

In many of these poems, criminal defendants receive a special measure of sympathy. In "You Felons on Trial in Courts," Walt Whitman indulges in a quintessentially Whitmanian act of imaginative generosity: "Who am I too that I am not on trial or in prison?" "In the Dock" by Walter de la Mare provides a more vivid and disturbing portrait of a "mis-shapen" murder defendant hauled from his "poisonous slum," standing in the dock and listening to the meaningless "drone" of legal language while the eyes of courtroom spectators swarm over him like flies on dead flesh. In Browning's *The Ring and the Book*, a far more articulate accused murderer speaks perhaps for a large proportion of defendants through time when he pleads to his judges, "Take my whole life, not this last act alone, / Look on it by the light reflected thence!" Finally, Alan Dugan's savagely surreal "Defendant" posits a fundamental sadism at the heart of the justice system.

POEMS ABOUT HISTORICAL TRIALS

Some of the most famous trials in British and American history are evoked in poems included here. Edmund Spenser in *The Faerie Queene* allegorizes the treason trial of Mary, Queen of Scots, assuring us of the rectitude of the proceedings and the just and merciful nature of Mary's royal opponent Elizabeth. Elsewhere, though, the poets sympathize with the defendants. "The Passionate Man's Pilgrimage," attributed to Sir Walter Raleigh, deals with

Raleigh's own treason trial, condemning its "forged accusers" and "bribed lawyer[s]" and anticipating his ultimate vindication by the one "unblotted lawyer," Christ, who pleads for all sinners before God. Stephen Vincent Benét's account of the trial of John Brown is dominated by Brown's own courtroom speech, which draws a similar contrast between the laws of God and man.

From a perspective sympathetic to the defendants, the trials of Mary, Raleigh, and Brown were all political trials masquerading as criminal proceedings. The same could be said of the 1920s trial of Sacco and Vanzetti, who, in the eyes of their many intellectual supporters, had been framed for robbery and murder because of their immigrant backgrounds and anarchist political views. Writing after the men were convicted and sentenced to death, Edna St. Vincent Millay ("Justice Denied in Massachusetts") and William Carlos Williams ("Impromptu: The Suckers") offer two very different poetic responses: the first quietly, bleakly despairing, the second fiercely vituperative. In the 1930s, the trial of the Scottsboro Boys will draw similar protests from American progressives, including the poets Langston Hughes and Muriel Rukeyser. In our selection, Hughes's powerfully condensed epigram "The Town of Scottsboro" is balanced by Rukeyser's "The Trial," with its sweeping evocation of the history of legal injustice, including the trials of John Brown and of Sacco and Vanzetti.

POEMS ABOUT PUNISHMENT (THE LAW'S HARD EDGE)

In his characteristically learned and witty poem "Tailor-Made," John Hollander asks, "How can a punishment fit a crime?" A number of other poets here implicitly raise the same question, though usually in more somber or angry tones. In "A Hymn to the Pillory," Daniel Defoe, who had been pilloried for writing an allegedly libelous pamphlet, offers a sardonic tribute to the instrument of his punishment. In *The Ballad of Reading Gaol,* Oscar Wilde similarly writes from his own bitter experience, protesting the injustice of his imprisonment at hard labor. Seamus Heaney ("Punishment") connects two different historical eras in order to offer a morally complex meditation on community, justice, and the spirit of revenge, while Thomas Lux considers the history of torture in "Traveling Exhibit of Torture Instruments." Also taking a long historical view is the nineteenth-century American poet John

Greenleaf Whittier, whose "The Gallows" attacks capital punishment as barbarous. Whittier's poem might have been conceived as an answer to *Sonnets upon the Punishment of Death* by his older English contemporary William Wordsworth. This little-known but fascinating sequence stands out as a rare literary defense of the death penalty, one that will give some readers a more complicated view of the character and legacy of the great Romantic. In the twentieth century, James Wright ("At the Executed Murderer's Grave") follows Whittier in condemning the death penalty, though he does so in more specifically modern tones of anguished uncertainty.

POEMS EXPLORING LEGAL CONCEPTS

The intellectual complexity of legal ideas has inspired poets to both serious and satirical reflections. In different periods and in different ways, Ralph Waldo Emerson ("Hamatreya") and Philip Levine ("Possession") explore the legal concept of property. William Empson ("Legal Fiction") constructs a dizzyingly metaphysical poem out of a *reductio ad absurdum* of certain doctrines in property law. Meanwhile Lawrence Joseph's elegantly elliptical and postmodern "Admissions against Interest" plays fruitfully with the meanings of the eponymous concept. William Matthews's dramatic monologue "Negligence" envisions a plaintiff's attorney offering a philosophical justification of tort law to a jury. Robert Hass's "The Woods in New Jersey" explores the subject of law more broadly, finding a striking organic metaphor to embody the philosophy that scholars would call legal realism. In "Law Like Love," W. H. Auden ranges even more widely, investigating the different potential meanings of the term "law" before coming to rest on the one that answers his sense of life most fully.

POEMS APPLYING LEGAL METAPHORS TO NONLEGAL SUBJECTS

Some of the most appealing and vibrant poems in this collection apply extended legal metaphors to nonlegal subjects. Renaissance sonneteers influenced by the Inns of Court, like Sir John Davies, apply extravagant legal conceits to the theme of love. As in Davies's "Into the Middle Temple of My Heart," it is sometimes hard to tell whether these poems are meant as specimens or parodies of a genre. Without sacrificing wit, Shakespeare adds a new profundity to this mode. His Sonnets 35 and 49 ask us to observe the ways in which unrequited love turns the lover into an advocate against himself, while Sonnet 134 elaborates a painful analogy between erotic obsession and the legal bonds of debt. In recent times, poets like Thom Gunn ("Legal Reform") and Glyn Maxwell ("The Sentence") have vigorously resurrected this tradition of the legalized love poem.

It may be asked what poems like this are doing in the present collection, if they are not, in the strictest sense, about the law. We would respond that each of these poems, by constructing elaborate legal metaphors, is always also implicitly conveying some vision of the law. Thus, Davies's "Middle Temple" draws attention to the structure of Renaissance legal education, while Shakespeare's Sonnet 35 points to the famous litigiousness of contemporary noblemen like the poet's beloved. Maxwell's "The Sentence" draws heavily on depictions of trials in popular films and novels and opens with a line that has the knowing force of a proverb: "Lied to like a judge I stepped down."

At their best, poems such as these enrich our sense of both life and law by uncovering hidden affinities between law and other important domains of human existence. Thus, Weldon Kees, in his sestina "After the Trial," deploys the language of the criminal law to describe the emotional burdens that families too often inflict on their members. Meanwhile, in his remarkable epigram "The Judge Is Fury," J. V. Cunningham draws a condensed but intricate analogy between law and literature, suggesting that the literary tradition is necessarily founded on acts of judging as formal and harsh as anything that occurs in a courtroom.

The poems that follow, presented in chronological order according to the date of birth of the poet, were selected for their aesthetic value, their relevance to the subject of law, and, to a smaller extent, their status as exhibits in both literary and legal history. It is the wish of the editors that this anthology find a diverse community of readers. We hope that scholars of law and literature will find in it considerable new matter worthy of study and that lawyers and law students will discover new perspectives on their chosen profession. We also hope that experienced readers of poetry will feel that the collection broadens their sense of poetry's thematic reach and shows them some favorite poets working in an unexpected vein. We further hope that some of the many readers devoted to legal fiction will pick up the book to discover that legal poetry, too, can convey much of the sheer human drama of the subject. Finally, we hope that it may inspire new poets—both lawyers and nonlawyers—to add to the growing canon of poems about the law.

A NOTE ON THE EDITING

Most of the pre-nineteenth-century poems in this anthology are presented in versions with modernized spelling, punctuation, and capitalization. Exceptions are the works by Chaucer, whose Middle English is a different language; Spenser, whose *Faerie Queene* employs archaic orthography for aesthetic effect; and the poems in Scots dialect by Dunbar, Fergusson, and Burns.

Obsolete, dialect, and foreign words are glossed in the notes at the end of the volume.

NOTES

1 Two collections of the last century—now long out of print—combined a smattering of genuine poetry with vast quantities of doggerel verse by amateur writers (mostly lawyers reflecting sentimentally or whimsically on their profession). See Ina Russell Warren, ed., *The Lawyer's Alcove: Poems by the Lawyer, for the Lawyer, and about the Lawyer* (New York: Doubleday, Page and Co., 1990) and Percival E. Jackson, ed., *Justice and the Law: An Anthology of Legal Poetry and Verse* (Charlottesville, VA: Michie, 1960).

2 James Boyd White, *The Legal Imagination: Studies in the Nature of Legal Thought and Expression* (Boston: Little, Brown, 1973).

3 James Boyd White is a fine literary critic with a special interest in poetry. In a long series of books and articles, he has argued that the study of poetry can make lawyers more sensitive and perceptive in their professional interactions and more effective as producers of legal texts. But he has not focused specifically on poetry about the law. In a parallel way, Thomas Grey's book about the lawyer-poet Wallace Stevens (*The Wallace Stevens Case: Law and the Practice of Poetry* [Cambridge: Harvard UP, 1991]) argues that an immersion in Stevens can train lawyers in more subtle and resourceful ways of thinking and arguing. Grey, however, acknowledges that Stevens's work never directly addresses legal subjects.

4 Richard A. Posner, *Law and Literature: Third Edition* (Cambridge: Harvard UP, 2009), 191n.

5 We have avoided excerpting passages from plays (even such obvious candidates as *The Merchant of Venice* and *Measure for Measure*) on the grounds that the drama constitutes a distinct genre that, as noted above, has already been the subject of much attention from scholars of law and literature.

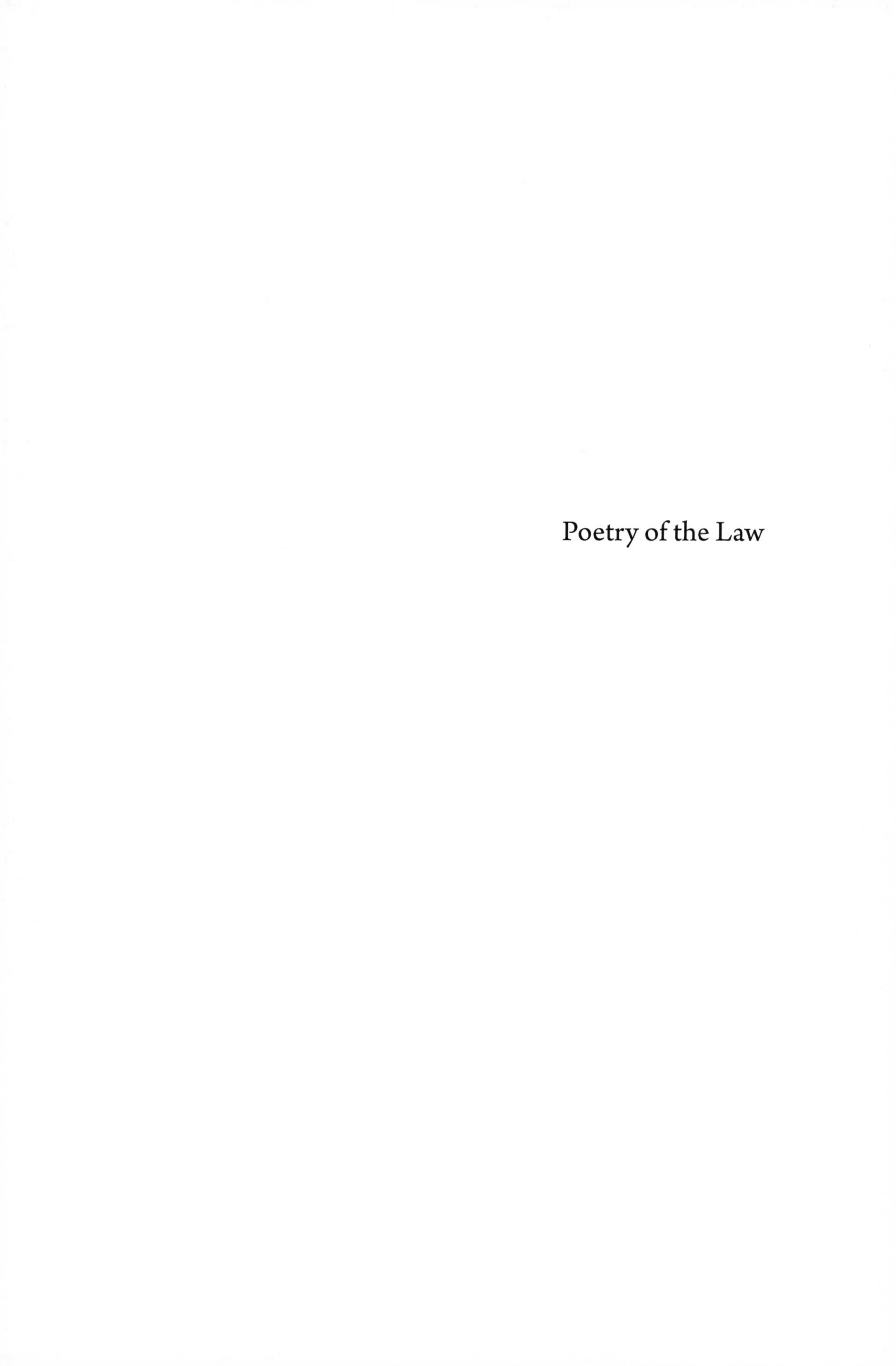

Poetry of the Law

Geoffrey Chaucer (c. 1343–1400)

from the general prologue to *The Canterbury Tales*

A Sergeant of the Lawe, war and wis,
That often hadde been at the Parvys
Ther was also, ful riche of excellence.
Discreet he was, and of greet reverence—
He seemed swich, his wordes weren so wise.
Justice he was ful often in assise
By patente and by plein commissioun.
For his science and for his heigh renown
Of fees and robes hadde he many oon.
So greet a purchasour was nowher noon;
Al was fee simple to him in effect—
His purchasing mighte nat been infect.
Nowher so bisy a man as he ther nas;
And yet he seemed bisier than he was.
In termes hadde he caas and doomes alle
That from the time of king William were falle.
Therto he coude endite and make a thing,
Ther coude no wight pinche at his writing;
And every statut coude he plein by rote.
He rood but hoomly in a medlee cote,
Girt with a ceint of silk, with barres smale.
Of his array telle I no lenger tale.

William Dunbar (1460–1530?)

Tydingis fra the Sessioun

Ane murlandis man of uplandis mak
At hame thus to his nychtbour spak,
"Quhat tydingis gossep, peax or weir?"
The tother rownit in his eir,
"I tell yow this undir confessioun,
Bot laitly lichtit of my meir
I come of Edinburch fra the Sessioun."

"Quhat tythingis hard ye thair, I pray yow?"
The tother answerit, "I sall say yow,
Keip this all secreit, gentill brother;
Is na man thair that trestis ane uther:
Ane commoun doar of transgressioun
Of innocent folkis prevenis a futher:
Sic tydingis hard I at the Sessioun."

Sum with his fallow rownis him to pleis,
That wald for invy byt of his neis;
His fa sum by the oxstar leidis;
Sum patteris with his mowth on beidis,
That hes his mynd all on oppressioun;
Sum beckis full law and schawis bair heidis,
Wald luke full heich war not the Sessioun.

Sum bydand the law layis land in wed;
Sum super expendit gois to his bed;
Sum speidis, for he in court hes menis;
Sum of parcialitie complenis;
How feid and favour flemis discretioun;
Sum speiks full fair, and falsly fenis:
Sic tythingis hard I at the Sessioun.

Sum castis summondis, and sum exceptis;
Sum standis besyd and skaild law keppis;
Sum is continuit, sum wynnis, sum tynis;
Sum makis him mirry at the wynis;
Sum is put owt of his possessioun;
Sum herreit, and on creddens dynis:
Sic tydingis hard I at the Sessioun.

Sum sweiris and forsaikis God;
Sum in ane lambskin is ane tod;
Sum in his toung his kyndnes tursis;
Sum cuttis throttis, and sum pykis pursis;
Sum gois to gallous with processioun;
Sum sanis the Sait, and sum thame cursis:
Sic tydingis hard I at the Sessioun.

Religious men of divers placis
Cumis thair to wow and se fair facis;
Baith Carmeleitis and Cordilleris
Cumis thair to genner and get ma freiris,
And ar unmyndfull of thair professioun;
The yungar at the eldar leiris:
Sic tydingis hard I at the Sessioun.

Thair cumis yung monkis of he complexioun,
Of devoit mynd, luve, and affectioun,
And in the courte thair hait flesche dantis,
Full faderlyk, with pechis and pantis;
Thay ar so humill of intercessioun,
All mercyfull wemen thair eirandis grantis:
Sic tydingis hard I at the Sessioun.

Edmund Spenser (c. 1552–1599)

from Book 5, Canto 9, *The Faerie Queene*

Then was there brought, as prisoner to the barre,
A Ladie of great countenance and place,
But that she it with foule abuse did marre;
Yet did appeare rare beautie in her face,
But blotted with condition vile and base,
That all her other honour did obscure,
And titles of nobilitie deface:
Yet in that wretched semblant, she did sure
The peoples great compassion unto her allure.

Then up arose a person of deepe reach,
And rare in-sight, hard matters to revele;
That well could charme his tongue, and time his speach
To all assayes; his name was called *Zele*:
He gan that Ladie strongly to appele
Of many haynous crymes, by her enured,
And with sharpe reasons rang her such a pele,
That those, whom she to pitie had allured,
He now t'abhorre and loath her person had procured.

First gan he tell, how this that seem'd so faire
And royally arayd, *Duessa* hight
That false *Duessa,* which had wrought great care,
And mickle mischiefe unto many a knight,
By her beguyled, and confounded quight:
But not for those she now in question came,
Though also those mote question'd be aright,
But for vyld treasons, and outrageous shame,
Which she against the dred *Mercilla* oft did frame.

For she whylome (as ye mote yet right well
Remember) had her counsels false conspyred,
With faithlesse *Blandamour* and *Paridell*,
(Both two her paramours, both by her hyred,
And both with hope of shadowes vaine inspyred,)
And with them practiz'd, how for to depryve
Mercilla of her crowne, by her aspyred,
That she might it unto her selfe deryve,
And tryumph in their blood, whom she to death did dryve.

But through high heavens grace, which favour not
The wicked driftes of trayterous desynes,
Gainst loiall Princes, all this cursed plot,
Ere proofe it tooke, discovered was betymes,
And th'actours won the meede meet for their crymes.
Such be the meede of all, that by such mene
Unto the type of kingdomes title clymes.
But false *Duessa* now untitled Queene,
Was brought to her sad doome, as here was to be seene.

Strongly did *Zele* her haynous fact enforce,
And many other crimes of foule defame
Against her brought, to banish all remorse,
And aggravate the horror of her blame.
And with him to make part against her, came
Many grave persons, that against her pled;
First was a sage old Syre, that had to name
The *Kingdomes care*, with a white silver hed,
That many high regards and reasons gainst her red.

Then gan *Authority* her to appose
With peremptorie powre, that made all mute;
And then the law of *Nations* gainst her rose,
And reasons brought, that no man could refute;
Next gan *Religion* gainst her to impute

High Gods beheast, and powre of holy lawes;
Then gan the Peoples cry and Commons sute,
Importune care of their owne publicke cause;
And lastly *Justice* charged her with breach of lawes.

But then for her, on the contrarie part,
Rose many advocates for her to plead:
First there came *Pittie,* with full tender hart,
And with her joyn'd *Regard* of womanhead;
And then came *Daunger* threatning hidden dread,
And high alliance unto forren powre;
Then came *Nobilitie* of birth, that bread
Great ruth through her misfortunes tragicke stowre;
And lastly *Griefe* did plead, and many teares forth powre.

With the neare touch whereof in tender hart
The Briton Prince was sore empassionate,
And woxe inclined much unto her part,
Through the sad terror of so dreadfull fate,
And wretched ruine of so high estate,
That for great ruth his courage gan relent.
Which when as *Zele* perceived to abate,
He gan his earnest fervour to augment,
And many fearefull objects to them to present.

He gan t'efforce the evidence anew,
And new accusements to produce in place:
He brought forth that old hag of hellish hew,
The cursed *Ate,* brought her face to face,
Who privie was, and partie in the case:
She, glad of spoyle and ruinous decay,
Did her appeach, and to her more disgrace,
The plot of all her practise did display,
And all her traynes, and all her treasons forth did lay.

Then brought he forth, with griesly grim aspect,
Abhorred *Murder,* who with bloudie knyfe
Yet dropping fresh in hand did her detect,
And there with guiltie bloudshed charged ryfe:
Then brought he forth *Sedition,* breeding stryfe
In troublous wits, and mutinous uprore:
Then brought he forth *Incontinence* of lyfe,
Even foule *Adulterie* her face before,
And lewd *Impietie,* that her accused sore.

All which when as the Prince had heard and seene,
His former fancies ruth he gan repent,
And from her partie eftsoones was drawen cleene.
But *Artegall* with constant firme intent,
For zeale of Justice was against her bent.
So was she guiltie deemed of them all.
Then *Zele* began to urge her punishment,
And to their Queene for judgement loudly call,
Unto *Mercilla* myld for Justice gainst the thrall.

But she, whose Princely breast was touched nere
With piteous ruth of her so wretched plight,
Though plaine she saw by all, that she did heare,
That she of death was guiltie found by right,
Yet would not let just vengeance on her light;
But rather let in stead thereof to fall
Few perling drops from her faire lampes of light;
The which she covering with her purple pall
Would have the passion hid, and up arose withall.

Sir Walter Raleigh (c. 1554–1618)

The Passionate Man's Pilgrimage

Give me my scallop-shell of quiet,
My staff of faith to walk upon,
My scrip of joy, immortal diet,
My bottle of salvation,
My gown of glory, hope's true gage,
And thus I'll take my pilgrimage.

Blood must be my body's balmer,
No other balm will there be given,
Whilst my soul like a white palmer
Travels to the land of heaven,
Over the silver mountains,
Where spring the nectar fountains;
And there I'll kiss
The bowl of bliss,
And drink my eternal fill
On every milken hill.
My soul will be a-dry before,
But after it will ne'er thirst more;
And by the happy blissful way
More peaceful pilgrims I shall see
That have shook off their gowns of clay
And go appareled fresh like me.
I'll bring them first
To slake their thirst,
And then to taste those nectar suckets,
At the clear wells
Where sweetness dwells,
Drawn up by saints in crystal buckets.

And when our bottles and all we
Are filled with immortality,
Then the holy paths we'll travel,
Strewed with rubies thick as gravel,
Ceilings of diamonds, sapphire floors,
High walls of coral, and pearl bowers,
From thence to heaven's bribeless hall
Where no corrupted voices brawl,
No conscience molten into gold,
Nor forged accusers bought and sold,
No cause deferred, nor vain-spent journey,
For there Christ is the king's attorney,
Who pleads for all, without degrees,
And he hath angels, but no fees.
When the grand twelve million jury
Of our sins and sinful fury,
'Gainst our souls black verdicts give,
Christ pleads his death, and then we live.
Be thou my speaker, taintless pleader,
Unblotted lawyer, true proceeder;
Thou movest salvation even for alms,
Not with a bribed lawyer's palms.
And this is my eternal plea
To him that made heaven, earth, and sea,
Seeing my flesh must die so soon,
And want a head to dine next noon,
Just at the stroke when my veins start and spread,
Set on my soul an everlasting head.
Then am I ready, like a palmer fit,
To tread those blest paths which before I writ.

William Shakespeare (1564–1616)

Sonnet 35

No more be griev'd at that which thou hast done:
Roses have thorns, and silver fountains mud;
Clouds and eclipses stain both moon and sun,
And loathsome canker lives in sweetest bud.
All men make faults, and even I in this,
Authorizing thy trespass with compare,
Myself corrupting, salving thy amiss,
Excusing thy sins more than thy sins are;
For to thy sensual fault I bring in sense—
Thy adverse party is thy advocate—
And 'gainst myself a lawful plea commence:
Such civil war is in my love and hate
    That I an accessary needs must be
    To that sweet thief which sourly robs from me.

William Shakespeare (1564–1616)

Sonnet 49

Against that time (if ever that time come)
When I shall see thee frown on my defects,
When as thy love hath cast his utmost sum,
Called to that audit by advis'd respects,
Against that time when thou shalt strangely pass,
And scarcely greet me with that sun thine eye,
When love converted from the thing it was
Shall reasons find of settled gravity,
Against that time do I ensconce me here
Within the knowledge of mine own desert,
And this my hand, against my self uprear,
To guard the lawful reasons on thy part.
    To leave poor me, thou hast the strength of laws,
    Since why to love, I can allege no cause.

William Shakespeare (1564–1616)

Sonnet 134

So now I have confessed that he is thine,
And I my self am mortgaged to thy will,
My self I'll forfeit, so that other mine,
Thou wilt restore to be my comfort still:
But thou wilt not, nor he will not be free,
For thou art covetous, and he is kind,
He learned but surety-like to write for me,
Under that bond that him as fast doth bind.
The statute of thy beauty thou wilt take,
Thou usurer that put'st forth all to use,
And sue a friend, came debtor for my sake,
So him I lose through my unkind abuse.
    Him have I lost, thou hast both him and me,
    He pays the whole, and yet am I not free.

Sir John Davies (1569–1626)

Into the Middle Temple of My Heart

Into the Middle Temple of my heart
The wanton Cupid did himself admit,
And gave for pledge your eagle-sighted wit
That he would play no rude uncivil part.
Long time he cloak'd his nature with his art,
And sad, and grave, and sober he did sit;
But at the last he 'gan to revel it,
To break good rules, and orders to pervert.
Then love and his young pledge were both convented
Before sad Reason, that old bencher grave,
Who this sad sentence unto him presented
By diligence, that sly and secret knave:
That love and wit for ever should depart
Out of the Middle Temple of my heart.

Ben Jonson (1572–1637)

An Epigram to the Counsellor

That I, hereafter, do not think the Bar
        The seat made of a more than civil war,
Or the Great Hall at Westminster the field
        Where mutual frauds are fought, and no side yield;
That, henceforth, I believe nor books nor men
        Who 'gainst the law weave calumnies, my [Benn],
But when I read or hear the names so rife
        Of hirelings, wranglers, stitchers-to of strife,
Hook-handed harpies, gowned vultures, put
        Upon the reverend pleaders; do now shut
All mouths that dare entitle them (from hence)
        To the wolf's study, or dog's eloquence:
Thou art my cause; whose manners since I knew,
        Have made me to conceive a lawyer new.
So dost thou study matter, men, and times,
        Mak'st it religion to grow rich by crimes;
Dar'st not abuse thy wisdom in the laws,
        Or skill, to carry out an evil cause,
But first dost vex and search it. If not sound,
        Thou prov'st the gentler ways to cleanse the wound,
And make the scar fair; if that will not be,
        Thou hast the brave scorn to put back the fee.
But in a business that will bide the touch,
        What use, what strength of reason! and how much
Of books, of precedents hast thou at hand!
        As if the general store thou didst command
Of argument, still drawing forth the best,
        And not being borrowed by thee, but possessed.
So com'st thou like a chief into the court,
        Armed at all pieces, as to keep a fort

Against a multitude, and (with thy style
        So brightly brandished) wound'st, defend'st—the while
Thy adversaries fall, as not a word
        They had, but were a reed unto thy sword.
Then com'st thou off with victory and palm,
        Thy hearers' nectar, and thy client's balm,
The court's just honour, and thy judge's love.
        And (which doth all achievements get above)
Thy sincere practice breeds not thee a fame
        Alone, but all thy rank a reverend name.

John Donne (1572–1631)

Satire 2

Sir, though (I thank God for it) I do hate
Perfectly all this town, yet there's one state
In all ill things so excellently best,
That hate, toward them, breeds pity towards the rest.
Though poetry indeed be such a sin
As I think that brings dearths, and Spaniards in,
Though like the pestilence or old fashion'd love,
It riddlingly catch men; and doth remove
Never, till it be starv'd out; yet their state
Is poor, disarm'd, like Papists, not worth hate:
One, (like a wretch, which at bar judg'd as dead,
Yet prompts him which stands next, and could not read,
And saves his life) gives idiot actors means
(Starving himself) to live by his labor'd scenes.
As in some organ, puppets dance above
And bellows pant below, which them do move.
One would move love by rhymes; but witchcraft's charms
Bring not now their old fears, nor their old harms:
Rams, and slings now are silly battery,
Pistolets are the best artillery.
And they who write to Lords, rewards to get,
Are they not like boys singing at doors for meat?
And they who write, because all write, have still
That excuse for writing, and for writing ill.
But he is worst, who (beggarly) doth chaw
Others' wits' fruits, and in his ravenous maw
Rankly digested, doth those things outspew,
As his own things; and they are his own, 'tis true,
For if one eat my meat, though it be known
The meat was mine, th'excrement is his own.
But these do me no harm, nor they which use

To out-swive dildos, and out-usure Jews;
To out-drink the sea, to out-swear the Litany;
Who with sins all kinds as familiar be
As confessors; and for whose sinful sake
Schoolmen new tenements in hell must make:
Whose strange sins, canonists could hardly tell
In which commandment's large receipt they dwell.
But these punish themselves; the insolence
Of Coscus only breeds my great offense,
Whom time (which rots all, and makes botches pox,
And plodding on, must make a calf an ox)
Hath made a lawyer, which was (alas) of late
But a scarce poet; jollier of this state,
Than are new benefic'd ministers, he throws
Like nets, or lime-twigs, wheresoe'er he goes,
His title of barrister, on every wench,
And woos in language of the pleas, and bench:
"A motion, Lady." "Speak Coscus." "I have been
In love, ever since *tricesimo* of the queen.
Continual claims I have made, injunctions got
To stay my rival's suit, that he should not
Proceed." "Spare me." "In Hillary term I went,
You said, If I return'd next 'size in Lent,
I should be in remitter of your grace;
In th'interim my letters should take place
Of affidavits." Words, words, which would tear
The tender labyrinth of a soft maid's ear,
More, more, than ten Sclavonians' scolding, more
Than when winds in our ruin'd abbeys roar.
When sick with poetry, and posses'd with Muse
Thou wast, and mad, I hop'd; but men which choose
Law practice for mere gain, bold soul, repute
Worse than imbrothel'd strumpets prostitute.
Now like an owl-like watchman, he must walk
His hand still at a bill, now he must talk
Idly, like prisoners, which whole months will swear

That only suretyship hath brought them there,
And to every suitor lie in every thing,
Like a king's favorite, yea like a king;
Like a wedge in a block, wring to the bar,
Bearing like asses, and more shameless far
Then carted whores, lie, to the grave judge; for
Bastardy abounds not in kings' titles, nor
Simony and sodomy in churchmen's lives,
As these things do in him; by these he thrives.
Shortly (as the sea) he will compass all our land;
From Scots, to Wight; from Mount, to Dover strand.
And spying heirs melting with luxury,
Satan will not joy at their sins, as he.
For as a thrifty wench scrapes kitchen stuff,
And barreling the droppings, and the snuff,
Of wasting candles, which in thirty year
(Relic-like kept) perchance buys wedding gear;
Piecemeal he gets lands, and spends as much time
Wringing each acre, as men pulling prime.
In parchments then, large as his fields, he draws
Assurances, big, as gloss'd civil laws,
So huge, that men (in our time's forwardness)
Are Fathers of the Church for writing less.
These he writes not; nor for these written pays,
Therefore spares no length; as in those first days
When Luther was profess'd, he did desire
Short *Pater nosters,* saying as a friar
Each day his beads, but having left those laws,
Adds to Christ's prayer, the power and glory clause.
But when he sells or changes land, he impairs
His writings, and (unwatch'd) leaves out, *ses heires,*
As slyly as any commenter goes by
Hard words, or sense; or in Divinity
As controverters, in vouch'd texts, leave out
Shrewd words, which might against them clear the doubt.
Where are those spread woods which cloth'd heretofore

These bought lands? not built, not burnt within door.
Where th'old landlord's troops, and alms? In great halls
Carthusian fasts, and fulsome Bacchanals
Equally I hate. Means bless. In rich men's homes
I bid kill some beasts, but no hecatombs,
None starve, none surfeit so; but oh, we allow
Good works as good, but out of fashion now,
Like old rich wardrobes. But my words none draws
Within the vast reach of th'huge statute laws.

John Donne (1572–1631)

Satire 5

Thou shalt not laugh in this leaf, Muse, nor they
Whom any pity warms. He which did lay
Rules to make courtiers, (he being understood
May make good courtiers, but who courtiers good?)
Frees from the stings of jests all who in extreme
Are wretch'd or wicked. Of these two a theme
Charity and liberty give me. What is he
Who officer's rage and suitor's misery
Can write and jest? If all things be in all,
(As I think, since all, which were, are, and shall
Be, be made of the same elements:
Each thing, each thing implies or represents.)
Then man is a world, in which, officers
Are the vast ravishing seas, and suitors,
Springs, now full, now shallow, now dry; which to
That which drowns them run. These self reasons do
Prove the world a man, in which officers
Are the devouring stomach, and suitors
Th'excrement which they void. All men are dust;
How much worse are suitors, who to men's lust
Are made preys? O worse than dust, or worm's meat,
For they do eat you now, whose selves worms shall eat.
They are the mills which grind you, yet you are
The wind which drives them; and a wasteful war
Is fought against you, and you fight it. They
Adulterate law, and you prepare their way
Like wittols; th'issue your own ruin is.
Greatest and fairest empress, know you this?
Alas, no more than Thames' calm head doth know
Whose meads her arms drown, or whose corn o'erflow.
You Sir, whose righteousness she loves, whom I

By having leave to serve, am most richly
For service paid, authoriz'd now, begin
To know and weed out this enormous sin.
O age of rusty iron! Some better wit
Call it some worse name, if ought equal it.
Th'Iron Age that was, when justice was sold; now
Injustice is sold dearer far. Allow
All claim'd fees, and duties; gamesters, anon
The money which you swear and sweat for is gone
Into other hands: So controverted lands
'Scape, like Angelica, the striver's hands.
If Law be in the judge's heart, and he
Have no heart to resist letter or fee,
Where wilt thou appeal? Power of the courts below
Flow from the first main head: and these can throw
Thee, if they suck thee in, to misery,
To fetters, halters; But if th'injury
Steel thee to dare complain, alas, thou go'st
Against the stream, when upwards: when thou art most
Heavy and most faint. And in those labors, they
'Gainst whom thou should'st complain, will in thy way
Become great seas, o'er which when thou shalt be
Forc'd to make golden bridges, thou shalt see
That all thy gold was drown'd in them before.
All things follow their likes; only who have, may have more.
Judges are gods; he who made and said them so,
Meant not men should be forc'd to them to go,
By means of angels. When supplications
We send to God, to Dominations,
Powers, Cherubins, and all heaven's courts, if we
Should pay fees, as here, daily bread would be
Scarce to kings; so 'tis. Would it not anger
A Stoic, a coward, yea a martyr,
To see a pursuivant come in, and call
All his clothes, copes, books, primers and all
His plate, chalices; and mistake them away,

And ask a fee for coming? Oh, ne'er may
Fair law's white reverend name be strumpeted,
To warrant thefts: she is established
Recorder to destiny on earth, and she
Speaks fate's words, and but tells us who must be
Rich, who poor, who in chains, who in jails.
She is all fair, but yet hath foul long nails,
With which she scratcheth suitors. In bodies
Of men, so in law, nails are th'extremities,
So officers stretch to more than law can do,
As our nails reach what no else part comes to.
Why bar'st thou to yon officer, fool? Hath he
Got those goods, for which erst men bar'd to thee?
Fool, twice, thrice, thou hast bought wrong, and now hungerly
Beg'st right; but that dole comes not till these die.
Thou hadst much, and law's Urim and Thummim try
Thou wouldst for more; and for all hast paper
Enough to clothe all the great Carrick's pepper.
Sell that, and by that thou much more shalt leese,
Than Haman, if he sold his antiquities.
O wretch, that thy fortunes should moralize
Aesop's fables, and make tales prophecies.
Thou art that swimming dog whom shadows cozened,
And div'dst, near drowning, for what vanished.

Bartholomew Griffin (c. 1570–1602)

Arraigned, Poor Captive

Arraigned, poor captive at the bar I stand,
The bar of beauty, bar to all my joys;
And up I hold my ever-trembling hand,
Wishing or life or death to end annoys.
And when the judge doth question of the guilt
And bids me speak, then sorrow shuts up words.
Yea, though he say, Speak boldly what thou wilt,
Yet my confused affects no speech affords.
For why, alas, my passions have no bound,
For fear of death that penetrates so near;
And still one grief another doth confound,
Yet doth at length a way to speech appear.
Then, for I speak too late, the judge doth give
His sentence that in prison I shall live.

Robert Herrick (1591–1674)

Upon Case

Case is a Lawyer, that ne'er pleads alone,
But when he hears the like confusion,
As when the disagreeing Commons throw
About their House, their clamorous Aye, or No:
Then Case, as loud as any serjeant there,
Cries out (my Lord, my Lord) the case is clear:
But when all's hushed, Case than a fish more mute,
Bestirs his hand, but starves in hand the suit.

Edward Taylor (c. 1642–1729)

Meditation 38: An Advocate with the Father

Oh! What a thing is man? Lord, who am I?
    That thou shouldst give him Law (Oh! golden line)
To regulate his thoughts, words, life thereby.
    And judge him wilt thereby too in thy time.
    A court of justice thou in heaven holdst
    To try his case while he's here housed on mold.

How do thy angels lay before thine eye
    My deeds both white, and black I daily do?
How doth thy court thou pannel'st there them try?
    But flesh complains. What right for this? let's know.
    For right or wrong I can't appear unto't.
    And shall a sentence pass on such a suit?

Soft; blemish not this golden bench, or place.
    Here is no bribe, nor colourings to hide
Nor pettifogger to befog the case
    But Justice hath her glory here well tried.
    Her spotless Law all spotted cases tends.
    Without respect or disrespect them ends.

God's judge himself: and Christ attorney is,
    The Holy Ghost registerer is found.
Angels the sergeants are, all creatures kiss
    The book, and do as evidences abound.
    All cases pass according to pure Law
    And in the sentence is no fret, nor flaw.

What say'st, my soul? Here all thy deeds are tried.
Is Christ thy advocate to plead thy cause?
Art thou his client? Such shall never slide.
He never lost his case: he pleads such laws
As carry do the same, nor doth refuse
The vilest sinner's case that doth him choose.

This is his honour, not dishonour: nay
No habeas corpus 'gainst his clients came;
For all their fines his purse doth make down pay.
He non-suits Satan's suit or casts the same.
He'll plead thy case, and not accept a fee.
He'll plead sub forma pauperis for thee.

My case is bad. Lord, be my advocate.
My sin is red: I'm under God's arrest.
Thou hast the hint of pleading; plead my state.
Although it's bad thy plea will make it best.
If thou wilt plead my case before the King:
I'll wagon loads of love, and glory bring.

Daniel Defoe (c. 1660–1731)

from "A Hymn to the Pillory"

What need of satire to reform the town?
   Or laws to keep our vices down?
   Let them to thee due homage pay,
This will reform us all *The Shortest Way.*
Let them to thee, bring all the knaves and fools,
   Virtue will guide the rest by rules;
They'll need no treacherous friends, no breach of faith,
No hired evidence with their infecting breath;
   No servants masters to betray,
   Or knights of the post, who swear for pay;
No injured author'll on thy steps appear,
Not such as *would* be rogues, but such as *are.*

   The first intent of laws
Was to correct the effect, and check the cause;
   And all the ends of punishment,
Were only future mischiefs to prevent.
   But justice is inverted when
         Those engines of the law,
Instead of pinching vicious men,
         Keep honest ones in awe;
   Thy business is, as all men know,
To punish villains, not to make men so.

   Whenever then, thou art prepared
To prompt that vice, thou should'st reward,
And by the terrors of thy grisly face
   Make men turn rogues to shun disgrace;
The end of thy creation is destroyed;
Justice expires of course, and law's made void.

What are thy terrors? that, for fear of thee,
Mankind should dare to sink their honesty?
He's bold to impudence that dare turn knave,
The scandal of thy company to save:
He that will crimes he never knew confess,
Does, more than if he know those crimes, transgress:
  And he that fears thee, more than to be base;
  May want a heart, but does not want a face.

  Thou like the devil dost appear,
Blacker than really thou art, by far:
  A wild chimeric notion of reproach;
Too little for a crime, for none too much.
  Let none th'indignity resent;
For crime is all the shame of punishment.

Thou bugbear of the law stand up and speak,
  Thy long misconstrued silence break,
Tell us, who 'tis, upon thy ridge stands there,
  So full of fault, and yet so void of fear;
  And from the paper in his hat,
  Let all mankind be told for what:

Tell them it was because he was too bold,
And told those truths which should not have been told.
  Extol the justice of the land,
Who punish what they will not understand.
  Tell them he stands exalted there
  For speaking what we would not hear;
  And yet he might have been secure,
Had he said less, or would he have said more.
  Tell them that this is his reward,
  And worse is yet for him prepared,
Because his foolish virtue was so nice,
As not to sell his friends, according to his friends' advice.

And thus he's an example made,
To make men of their honesty afraid;
That for the time to come, they may
More willingly, their friends betray;
Tell them, the men that placed him here,
Are scandals to the times,
Are at a loss to find his guilt,
And can't commit his crimes.

Jonathan Swift (1667–1745)

The Answer to "Paulus"

PAULUS, BY MR. LINDSAY

A slave to crowds, scorched with the summer's heats,
In court the wretched lawyer toils, and sweats:
While smiling nature, in her best attire,
Doth soothe each sense, and joy and love inspire.
Can he who knows, that real good should please,
Barter for gold his liberty and ease?
Thus Paulus preached: when entering at the door,
Upon his board a client pours the ore:
He grasps the shining gift, pores o'er the cause,
Forgets the sun, and dozes on the laws.

THE ANSWER, BY DR. SWIFT

Lindsay mistakes the matter quite,
And honest Paulus judges right.
Then, why these quarrels to the sun,
Without whose aid you're all undone?
Did Paulus e'er complain of sweat?
Did Paulus e'er the sun forget?
The influence of whose golden beams
Soon licks up all unsavoury steams;
The sun, you say, his face has kissed:
It has; but then it greased his fist.
True lawyers, for the wisest ends,
Have always been Apollo's friends;
Not for his superficial powers
Of ripening fruits, and gilding flowers;
Not for inspiring poets' brains
With pennyless and starveling strains;

Not for his boasted healing art;
Not for his skill to shoot the dart;
Nor yet, because he sweetly fiddles;
Nor for his prophecies in riddles:
But for a more substantial cause:
Apollo's patron of the laws;
Whom Paulus ever must adore,
As parent of the golden ore,
By Phoebus (an incestuous birth)
Begot upon his grandam Earth;
By Phoebus first produced to light:
By Vulcan formed so round and bright:
Then offered at the throne of justice,
By clients to her priests and trustees.
Nor when we see Astraea stand
With equal balance in her hand,
Must we suppose she has in view,
How to give every man his due:
Her scales you only see her hold
To weigh her priests', the lawyers', gold.
Now, should I own your case was grievous,
Poor sweaty Paulus, who'd believe us?

'Tis very true, and none denies,
At least, that such complaints are wise:
'Tis wise, no doubt, as clients fat ye more,
To cry, like statesmen, *quanta patimur*!
But, since the truth must needs be stretched
To prove, that lawyers are so wretched;
This paradox I'll undertake
For Paulus' and for Lindsay's sake
By topics, which though I abomine 'em,
May serve, as arguments *ad hominem*.
Yet I disdain to offer those,
Made use of by detracting foes.

I own, the curses of mankind
Sit light upon a lawyer's mind:
The clamours of ten thousand tongues
Break not his rest, nor hurt his lungs:
I own his conscience always free,
(Provided he has got a fee.)
Secure of constant peace within,
He knows no guilt, who knows no sin.

Yet well they merit to be pitied,
By clients always overwitted.
And, though the gospel seems to say,
What heavy burdens lawyers lay
Upon the shoulders of their neighbour,
Nor lend a finger to the labour,
Always for saving their own bacon:
No doubt the text is here mistaken:
The copy's false, and sense is racked:
To prove it I appeal to fact;
And thus by demonstration show,
What burdens lawyers undergo.

With early clients at his door,
Though he were drunk the night before,
And crop-sick with unclubbed-for wine,
The wretch must be at court by nine:
Half sunk beneath his brief and bag,
As ridden by a midnight hag:
Then, from the bar, harangues the bench
In English vile, and viler French,
And Latin, vilest of the three:
And all for ten poor moidores' fee!
Of paper how he is profuse,
With periods long, in terms abstruse!
What pains he takes to be prolix!
A thousand words to stand for six!

Of common sense without a word in!
And is this not a grievous burden?

The lawyer is a common drudge,
To fight our cause before the judge:
And, what is yet a greater curse,
Condemned to bear his client's purse;
While he, at ease, secure and light,
Walks boldly home at dead of night;
When term is ended, leaves the town,
Trots to his country mansion down;
And, disencumbered of his load,
No danger dreads upon the road;
Despises rapparees, and rides
Safe through the Newry mountain sides.

Lindsay, 'tis you have set me on
To state the question *pro* and *con*:
My satire may offend, 'tis true:
However, it concerns not you.
I own, there may in every clan
Perhaps be found one honest man:
Yet link them close; in this they jump,
To be but rascals in the lump.
Imagine Lindsay at the bar:
He's just the same, his brethren are;
Well taught by practice to imbibe
The fundamentals of his tribe;
And, in his client's just defence,
Must deviate oft from common sense,
And make his ignorance discerned,
To get the name of council learned;
(As *lucus* comes *a non lucendo*)
And wisely do as other men do.
But, shift him to a better scene,
Got from his crew of rogues in grain;

Surrounded with companions fit
To taste his humour, and his wit;
You'd swear, he never took a fee,
Nor knew in law his A B C.

'Tis hard, where dullness overrules,
To keep good sense in crowds of fools;
And we admire the man, who saves
His honesty in crowds of knaves;
Nor yields up virtue, at discretion,
To villains of his own profession.
Lindsay, you know, what pains you take
In both, yet hardly save your stake.
And will you venture both anew?
To sit among that scoundrel crew,
That pack of mimic legislators,
Abandoned, stupid, slavish praters!
For, as the rabble daub, and rifle
The fool, who scrambles for a trifle;
Who for his pains is cuffed, and kicked,
Drawn through the dirt, his pockets picked;
You must expect the like disgrace,
Scrambling with rogues to get a place:
Must lose the honour you have gained,
Your numerous virtues foully stained;
Disclaim forever all pretence
To common honesty and sense;
And join in friendship, with a strict tie,
To Marshall, Conolly, and Dick Tighe.

Alexander Pope (1688–1744)

Verbatim from Boileau

Once (says an author; where, I need not say)
Two trav'lers found an oyster in their way;
Both fierce, both hungry; the dispute grew strong,
While scale in hand Dame Justice past along.
Before her each with clamour pleads the laws,
Explain'd the matter, and would win the cause.
Dame Justice, weighing long the doubtful right,
Takes, opens, swallows it, before their sight.
The cause of strife remov'd so rarely well,
"There take" (says Justice) "take ye each a shell
We thrive at Westminster on fools like you:
'Twas a fat oyster—live in peace—Adieu."

Sir William Blackstone (1723–1780)

The Lawyer's Farewell to His Muse

As, by some tyrant's stern command,
A wretch forsakes his native land,
In foreign climes condemn'd to roam
An endless exile from his home;
Pensive he treads the destined way,
And dreads to go; nor dares to stay;
Till on some neighbouring mountain's brow
He stops, and turns his eyes below;
There, melting at the well-known view,
Drops a last tear, and bids adieu:
So I, thus doom'd from thee to part,
Gay queen of Fancy, and of Art,
Reluctant move, with doubtful mind,
Oft stop, and often look behind.

Companion of my tender age,
Serenely gay, and sweetly sage,
How blithsome were we wont to rove
By verdant hill, or shady grove,
Where fervent bees, with humming voice,
Around the honey'd oak rejoice,
And aged elms with awful bend
In long cathedral walks extend!
Lull'd by the lapse of gliding floods,
Cheer'd by the warbling of the woods,
How blest my days, my thoughts how free,
In sweet society with thee!
Then all was joyous, all was young,
And years unheeded roll'd along:
But now the pleasing dream is o'er,

These scenes must charm me now no more.
Lost to the fields, and torn from you,—
Farewell!—a long, a last adieu.
Me wrangling courts, and stubborn law,
To smoke, and crowds, and cities draw:
There selfish faction rules the day,
And pride and avarice throng the way;
Diseases taint the murky air,
And midnight conflagrations glare;
Loose Revelry, and Riot bold
In frighted streets their orgies hold;
Or, where in silence all is drown'd,
Fell Murder walks his lonely round;
No room for peace, no room for you,
Adieu, celestial nymph, adieu!

Shakspeare no more, thy sylvan son,
Nor all the art of Addison,
Pope's heaven strung lyre, nor Waller's ease,
Nor Milton's mighty self must please:
Instead of these a formal band
In furs, and coifs around me stand;
With sounds uncouth and accents dry,
That grate the soul of harmony,
Each pedant sage unlocks his store
Of mystic, dark, discordant lore;
And points with tottering hand the ways
That lead me to the thorny maze.

There, in a winding close retreat,
Is justice doom'd to fix her seat;
There, fenced by bulwarks of the law,
She keeps the wondering world in awe;
And there, from vulgar sight retired,
Like eastern queens, is more admired.

O let me pierce the secret shade
Where dwells the venerable maid!
There humbly mark, with reverent awe,
The guardian of Britannia's law;
Unfold with joy her sacred page,
The united boast of many an age;
Where mix'd, yet uniform, appears
The wisdom of a thousand years.
In that pure spring the bottom view,
Clear, deep, and regularly true;
And other doctrines thence imbibe
Than lurk within the sordid scribe;
Observe how parts with parts unite
In one harmonious rule of right;
See countless wheels distinctly tend
By various laws to one great end:
While mighty Alfred's piercing soul
Pervades, and regulates the whole.

Then welcome business, welcome strife,
Welcome the cares, the thorns of life,
The visage wan, the pore-blind sight,
The toil by day, the lamp at night,
The tedious forms, the solemn prate,
The pert dispute, the dull debate,
The drowsy bench, the babbling Hall,
For thee, fair Justice, welcome all!
Thus though my noon of life be past,
Yet let my setting sun, at last,
Find out the still, the rural cell,
Where sage Retirement loves to dwell!
There let me taste the homefelt bliss
Of innocence, and inward peace;
Untainted by the guilty bribe,
Uncursed amid the harpy tribe;

No orphan's cry to wound my ear;
My honour, and my conscience clear;
Thus may I calmly meet my end,
Thus to the grave in peace descend.

William Cowper (1731–1800)

The Cause Won

Two neighbours furiously dispute,
A field the subject of the suit;
Trivial the spot—yet such the rage
With which the combatants engage,
'Twere hard to tell who covets most
The prize, at whatsoever cost.
The pleadings swell. Words still suffice;
No single word but has its price;
No term but yields some fair pretence
For novel and increased expence.

Defendant, thus, becomes a name
Which he that bore it may disclaim,
Since both, in one description blended,
Are plaintiffs when the suit is ended.

Robert Fergusson (1750–1774)

The Rising of the Session

To a' men living be it kend,
The Session now is at an end:
Writers, your finger-nebbs unbend,
And quat the pen,
Till Time wi' lyart pow shall send
Blythe June again.

Tir'd o' the law, and a' its phrases,
The wylie writers, rich as Croesus,
Hurl frae the town in hackney chaises,
For country cheer:
The powny that in spring-time grazes,
Thrives a' the year.

Ye lawyers, bid fareweel to lies,
Fareweel to din, fareweel to fees,
The canny hours o' rest may please
Instead o' siller:
Hain'd multer hads the mill at ease,
And finds the miller.

Blyth they may be wha wanton play
In fortune's bonny blinkin ray,
Fu' weel can they ding dool away
Wi' comrades couthy,
And never dree a hungert day,
Or e'ening drouthy.

Ohon the day for him that's laid,
In dowie poortith's caldrife shade,

Ablins o'er honest for his trade,
He racks his wits,
How he may get his buick weel clad,
And fill his guts.

The farmers' sons, as yap as sparrows,
Are glad, I trow, to flee the barras,
And whistle to the plough and harrows
At barley seed:
What writer wadna gang as far as
He cou'd for bread.

After their yokin, I wat weel
They'll stoo the kebbuck to the heel;
Eith can the plough-stilts gar a chiel
Be unco vogie,
Clean to lick aff his crowdy-meal,
And scart his cogie.

Now mony a fallow's dung adrift
To a' the blasts beneath the lift,
And tho' their stamack's aft in tift
In vacance time,
Yet seenil do they ken the rift
O' stappit weym.

Now gin a Notar shou'd be wanted,
You'll find the pillars gayly planted;
For little thing *protests* are granted
Upo' a bill,
And weightiest matters covenanted
For haf a gill.

Nae body takes a morning dribb
O' Holland gin frae Robin Gibb;

And tho' a dram to Rob's mair sib
Than is his wife,
He maun take time to daut his Rib
Till siller's rife.

This vacance is a heavy doom
On Indian Peter's coffee-room,
For a' his china pigs are toom;
Nor do we see
In wine the sucker biskets soom
As light's a flee.

But stop, my Muse, nor make a main,
Pate disna fend on that alane;
He can fell twa dogs wi' ae bane,
While ither fock
Maun rest themselves content wi' ane,
Nor farer trock.

Ye change-house keepers never grumble,
Tho' you a while your bickers whumble,
Be unco patientfu' and humble,
Nor make a din,
Tho' gude joot binna kend to rumble
Your weym within.

You needna grudge to draw your breath
For little mair than haf a reath,
Than, gin we a' be spar'd frae death.
We'll gladly prie
Fresh noggans o' your reaming graith
Wi' blythsome glee.

George Crabbe (1754–1832)

from "Professions—Law"

The trader, grazier, merchant, priest and all,
Whose sons aspiring, for professions call,
Choose from their lads some bold and subtle boy,
And judge him fitted for this grave employ:
Him a keen old practitioner admits,
To write five years and exercise his wits:
The youth has heard—it is in fact his creed,
Mankind dispute, that lawyers may be fee'd:
Jails, bailiffs, writs, all terms and threats of law,
Grow now familiar as once top and taw;
Rage, hatred, fear, the mind's severer ills,
All bring employment, all augment his bills;
As feels the surgeon for the mangled limb,
The mangled mind is but a job for him;
Thus taught to think, these legal reasoners draw
Morals and maxims from their views of law;
They cease to judge by precepts taught in schools,
By man's plain sense, or by religious rules;
No! nor by law itself, in truth discern'd,
But as its statutes may be warp'd and turn'd;
How they should judge of man; his word and deed,
They in their books and not their bosoms read:
Of some good act you speak with just applause,
"No! no!" says he, "'twould be a losing cause:"
Blame you some tyrant's deed?—he answers, "Nay,
He'll get a verdict; heed you what you say."
Thus to conclusions from examples led,
The heart resigns all judgment to the head;
Law, law alone, for ever kept in view,
His measures guides, and rules his conscience too:
Of ten commandments, he confesses three

Are yet in force, and tells you which they be,
As law instructs him; thus: "Your neighbour's wife
You must not take, his chattels, nor his life;
Break these decrees, for damage you must pay,
These you must reverence, and the rest—you may."

Law was design'd to keep a state in peace;
To punish robbery, that wrong might cease;
To be impregnable; a constant fort,
To which the weak and injur'd might resort:
But these perverted minds its force employ,
Not to protect mankind, but to annoy;
And long as ammunition can be found,
Its lightning flashes and its thunders sound.

Or law with lawyers is an ample still,
Wrought by the passions' heat with chymic skill;
While the fire burns, the gains are quickly made,
And freely flow the profits of the trade;
Nay, when the fierceness fails, these artists blow
The dying fire, and make the embers glow,
As long as they can make the smaller profits flow;
At length the process of itself will stop,
When they perceive they've drawn out every drop.

Yet I repeat, there are, who nobly strive
To keep the sense of moral worth alive;
Men who would starve, ere meanly deign to live
On what deception and chican'ry give;
And these at length succeed; they have their strife,
Their apprehensions, stops and rubs in life;
But honour, application, care, and skill,
Shall bend opposing fortune to their will.

Of such is *Archer*, he who keeps in awe
Contending parties by his threats of law:

He, roughly honest, has been long a guide
In borough-business, on the conquering side;
And seen so much of both sides, and so long,
He thinks the bias of man's mind goes wrong:
Thus, though he's friendly, he is still severe,
Surly though kind, suspiciously sincere:
So much he's seen of baseness in the mind,
That, while a friend to man, he scorns mankind;
He knows the human heart, and sees with dread,
By slight temptation, how the strong are led;
He knows how interest can asunder rend
The bond of parent, master, guardian, friend,
To form a new and a degrading tie
'Twixt needy vice and tempting villainy.
Sound in himself, yet when such flaws appear,
He doubts of all, and learns that self to fear;
For where so dark the moral view is grown,
A timid conscience trembles for her own;
The pitchy-taint of general vice is such
As daubs the fancy, and you dread the touch.

Robert Burns (1759–1796)

Extempore in the Court of Session

LORD ADVOCATE

He clenched his pamphlet in his fist,
He quoted and he hinted,
Till, in a declamation-mist,
His argument he tint it:
He gapèd for't, he grapèd for't,
He fand it was awa, man;
But what his common sense came short,
He ekèd out wi' law, man.

MR. ERSKINE

Collected, Harry stood awee,
Then open'd out his arm, man;
His Lordship sat wi' ruefu' e'e,
And ey'd the gathering storm, man:
Like wind-driven hail it did assail,
Or torrents owre a linn, man:
The bench sae wise, lift up their eyes,
Half-wauken'd wi' the din, man.

William Wordsworth (1770–1850)

from Sonnets upon the Punishment of Death

IV

Is *Death,* when evil against good has fought
With such fell mastery that a man may dare
By deeds the blackest purpose to lay bare—
Is Death, for one to that condition brought,—
For him, or any one,—the thing that ought
To be *most* dreaded? Lawgivers, beware,
Lest, capital pains remitting till ye spare
The murderer, ye, by sanction to that thought,
Seemingly given, debase the general mind;
Tempt the vague will tried standards to disown;
Nor only palpable restraints unbind,
But upon Honour's head disturb the crown,
Whose absolute rule permits not to withstand
In the weak love of life his least command.

William Wordsworth (1770–1850)

from Sonnets upon the Punishment of Death

VI

Ye brood of conscience—Spectres! that frequent
The bad man's restless walk, and haunt his bed—
Fiends in your aspect, yet beneficent
In act, as hovering Angels when they spread
Their wings to guard the unconscious Innocent—
Slow be the Statutes of the land to share
A laxity that could not but impair
Your power to punish crime, and so prevent.
And ye, Beliefs! coiled serpent-like about
The adage on all tongues, "Murder will out,"
How shall your ancient warnings work for good
In the full might they hitherto have shown,
If for deliberate shedder of man's blood.
Survive not Judgment that requires his own?

William Wordsworth (1770–1850)

from Sonnets upon the Punishment of Death

VIII

Fit retribution, by the moral code
Determined, lies beyond the State's embrace,
Yet, as she may, for each peculiar case
She plants well-measured terrors in the road
Of wrongful acts. Downward it is and broad,
And, the main fear once doomed to banishment,
Far oftener then, bad ushering worse event,
Blood would be spilt that in his dark abode
Crime might lie better hid. And, should the change
Take from the horror due to a foul deed,
Pursuit and evidence so far must fail,
And, guilt escaping, passion then might plead
In angry spirits for her old free range,
And the "wild justice of revenge" prevail.

William Wordsworth (1770–1850)

from Sonnets upon the Punishment of Death

XI

Ah, think how one compelled for life to abide
Locked in a dungeon needs must eat the heart
Out of his own humanity, and part
With every hope that mutual cares provide;
And, should a less unnatural doom confide
In life-long exile on a savage coast,
Soon the relapsing penitent may boast
Of yet more heinous guilt, with fiercer pride.
Hence thoughtful Mercy, Mercy sage and pure,
Sanctions the forfeiture that Law demands,
Leaving the final issue in *His* hands
Whose goodness knows no change, whose love is sure,
Who sees, foresees; who cannot judge amiss,
And wafts at will the contrite soul to bliss.

George Gordon, Lord Byron (1788–1824)

from Canto 10, *Don Juan*

The lawyer and the critic but behold
  The baser sides of literature and life,
And nought remains unseen, but much untold,
  By those who scour those double vales of strife.
While common men grow ignorantly old,
  The lawyer's brief is like the surgeon's knife,
Dissecting the whole inside of a question,
And with it all the process of digestion.

A legal broom's a moral chimney-sweeper,
  And that's the reason he himself's so dirty:
The endless soot bestows a tint far deeper
  Than can be hid by altering his shirt; he
Retains the sable stains of the dark creeper,
  At least some twenty-nine do out of thirty,
In all their habits:—Not so *you,* I own;
As Caesar wore his robe you wear your gown.

Percy Bysshe Shelley (1792–1822)

To the Lord Chancellor

1

Thy country's curse is on thee, darkest crest
  Of that foul, knotted, many-headed worm
Which rends our Mother's bosom—Priestly Pest!
  Masked Resurrection of a buried Form!

2

Thy country's curse is on thee! Justice sold,
  Truth trampled, Nature's landmarks overthrown,
And heaps of fraud-accumulated gold,
  Plead, loud as thunder, at Destruction's throne.

3

And, whilst that slow sure Angel which aye stands
  Watching the beck of Mutability
Delays to execute her high commands,
  And, though a nation weeps, spares thine and thee,

4

Oh, let a father's curse be on thy soul,
  And let a daughter's hope be on thy tomb;
Be both, on thy grey head, a leaden cowl
  To weigh thee down to thine approaching doom!

5

I curse thee by a parent's outraged love,
  By hopes long cherished and too lately lost,
By gentle feelings thou couldst never prove,
  By griefs which thy stern nature never crossed;

6

By those infantine smiles of happy light,
  Which were a fire within a stranger's hearth,
Quenched even when kindled, in untimely night
  Hiding the promise of a lovely birth;

7

By those unpractised accents of young speech,
  Which he who is a father thought to frame
To gentlest lore, such as the wisest teach—
  Thou strike the lyre of mind!—Oh, grief and shame!

8

By all the happy see in children's growth,
  That undeveloped flower of budding years,
Sweetness and sadness interwoven both,
  Source of the sweetest hopes and saddest fears;

9

By all the days, under a hireling's care,
  Of dull constraint and bitter heaviness,—
O wretched ye if ever any were,—
  Sadder than orphans, yet not fatherless!—

10

By the false cant which on their innocent lips
  Must hang like poison on an opening bloom;
By the dark creeds which cover with eclipse
  Their pathway from the cradle to the tomb;

11

By thy impious Hell, and all its terror;
  By all the grief, the madness, and the guilt

Of thine impostures, which must be their error—
  That sand on which thy crumbling power is built;

12

By thy complicity with lust and hate,
  Thy thirst for tears, thy hunger after gold,
The ready frauds which ever on thee wait,
  The servile arts in which thou hast grown old;

13

By thy most killing sneer, and by thy smile,
  By all the snares and nets of thy black den,
And—for thou canst outweep the crocodile—
  By thy false tears, those millstones braining men;

14

By all the hate which checks a father's love;
  By all the scorn which kills a father's care;
By those most impious hands which dared remove
  Nature's high bounds; by thee; and by despair—

15

Yes, the despair which bids a father groan,
  And cry, "My children are no longer mine;
The blood within those veins may be mine own,
  But, Tyrant, their polluted souls are thine!"—

16

I curse thee—though I hate thee not.—O slave!
  If thou couldst quench that earth-consuming Hell
Of which thou art a daemon, on thy grave
  This curse should be a blessing. Fare thee well!

Ralph Waldo Emerson (1803–1882)

Hamatreya

Bulkeley, Hunt, Willard, Hosmer, Meriam, Flint,
Possessed the land which rendered to their toil
Hay, corn, roots, hemp, flax, apples, wool and wood.
Each of these landlords walked amidst his farm,
Saying, "'T is mine, my children's and my name's.
How sweet the west wind sounds in my own trees!
How graceful climb those shadows on my hill!
I fancy these pure waters and the flags
Know me, as does my dog: we sympathize;
And, I affirm, my actions smack of the soil."

Where are these men? Asleep beneath their grounds:
And strangers, fond as they, their furrows plough.
Earth laughs in flowers, to see her boastful boys
Earth-proud, proud of the earth which is not theirs;
Who steer the plough, but cannot steer their feet
Clear of the grave.
They added ridge to valley, brook to pond,
And sighed for all that bounded their domain;
"This suits me for a pasture; that's my park;
We must have clay, lime, gravel, granite-ledge,
And misty lowland, where to go for peat.
The land is well,—lies fairly to the south.
'Tis good, when you have crossed the sea and back,
To find the sitfast acres where you left them."
Ah! the hot owner sees not Death, who adds
Him to his land, a lump of mould the more.
Hear what the Earth says:—

"Mine and yours;
Mine, not yours.
Earth endures;
Stars abide—
Shine down in the old sea;
Old are the shores;
But where are old men?
I who have seen much,
Such have I never seen.

"The lawyer's deed
Ran sure,
In tail,
To them, and to their heirs
Who shall succeed,
Without fail,
Forevermore.

"Here is the land,
Shaggy with wood,
With its old valley,
Mound and flood.
But the heritors?—
Fled like the flood's foam.
The lawyer, and the laws,
And the kingdom,
Clean swept herefrom.

"They called me theirs,
Who so controlled me;
Yet every one
Wished to stay, and is gone,
How am I theirs,

If they cannot hold me,
But I hold them?”

When I heard the Earth-song
I was no longer brave;
My avarice cooled
Like lust in the chill of the grave.

John Greenleaf Whittier (1807–1892)

The Gallows

I

The suns of eighteen centuries have shone
Since the Redeemer walked with man, and made
The fisher's boat, the cavern's floor of stone,
And mountain moss, a pillow for His head;
And He, who wandered with the peasant Jew,
And broke with publicans the bread of shame,
And drank with blessings, in His Father's name,
The water which Samaria's outcast drew,
Hath now His temples upon every shore,
Altar and shrine and priest; and incense dim
Evermore rising, with low prayer and hymn,
From lips which press the temple's marble floor,
Or kiss the gilded sign of the dread cross He bore.

II

Yet as of old, when, meekly "doing good,"
He fed a blind and selfish multitude,
And even the poor companions of His lot
With their dim earthly vision knew Him not,
How ill are His high teachings understood!
Where He hath spoken Liberty, the priest
At His own altar binds the chain anew;
Where He hath bidden to Life's equal feast,
The starving many wait upon the few;
Where He hath spoken Peace, His name hath been
The loudest war-cry of contending men;
Priests, pale with vigils, in His name have blessed
The unsheathed sword, and laid the spear in rest,
Wet the war-banner with their sacred wine,
And crossed its blazon with the holy sign;

Yea, in His name who bade the erring live,
And daily taught His lesson, to forgive!
    Twisted the cord and edged the murderous steel;
And, with His words of mercy on their lips,
Hung gloating o'er the pincers' burning grips,
    And the grim horror of the straining wheel;
Fed the slow flame which gnawed the victim's limb,
Who saw before his searing eyeballs swim
    The image of their Christ in cruel zeal,
Through the black torment-smoke, held mockingly to him!

III

The blood which mingled with the desert sand,
    And beaded with its red and ghastly dew
The vines and olives of the Holy Land;
    The shrieking curses of the hunted Jew;
The white-sown bones of heretics, where'er
They sank beneath the Crusade's holy spear,
Goa's dark dungeons, Malta's sea-washed cell,
    Where with the hymns the ghostly fathers sung
    Mingled the groans by subtle torture wrung,
Heaven's anthem blending with the shriek of hell!
The midnight of Bartholomew, the stake
    Of Smithfield, and that thrice-accursed flame
Which Calvin kindled by Geneva's lake;
New England's scaffold, and the priestly sneer
Which mocked its victims in that hour of fear,
    When guilt itself a human tear might claim,—
Bear witness, O Thou wronged and merciful One!
That Earth's most hateful crimes have in Thy name been done!

IV

Thank God! that I have lived to see the time
    When the great truth begins at last to find
    An utterance from the deep heart of mankind,

Earnest and clear, that all Revenge is Crime,
That man is holier than a creed, that all
        Restraint upon him must consult his good,
Hope's sunshine linger on his prison wall,
        And Love look in upon his solitude.
The beautiful lesson which our Saviour taught
Through long, dark centuries its way hath wrought
Into the common mind and popular thought;
And words, to which by Galilee's lake shore
The humble fishers listened with hushed oar,
Have found an echo in the general heart,
And of the public faith become a living part.

V

Who shall arrest this tendency? Bring back
The cells of Venice and the bigot's rack?
Harden the softening human heart again
To cold indifference to a brother's pain?
Ye most unhappy men! who, turned away
From the mild sunshine of the Gospel day,
        Grope in the shadows of Man's twilight time,
What mean ye, that with ghoul-like zest ye brood,
O'er those foul altars streaming with warm blood,
        Permitted in another age and clime?
Why cite that law with which the bigot Jew
Rebuked the Pagan's mercy, when he knew
No evil in the Just One? Wherefore turn
To the dark, cruel past? Can ye not learn
From the pure Teacher's life how mildly free
Is the great Gospel of Humanity?
The Flamen's knife is bloodless, and no more
Mexitli's altars soak with human gore,
No more the ghastly sacrifices smoke
Through the green arches of the Druid's oak;
And ye of milder faith, with your high claim

Of prophet-utterance in the Holiest name,
Will ye become the Druids of our time!
Set up your scaffold-altars in our land,
And, consecrators of Law's darkest crime,
        Urge to its loathsome work the hangman's hand?
Beware, lest human nature, roused at last,
From its peeled shoulder your encumbrance cast,
        And, sick to loathing of your cry for blood,
Rank ye with those who led their victims round
The Celt's red altar and the Indian's mound,
        Abhorred of Earth and Heaven, a pagan brotherhood!

Robert Browning (1812–1889)

from Book 5, *The Ring and the Book*

But now
Health is returned, and sanity of soul
Nowise indifferent to the body's harm.
I find the instinct bids me save my life;
My wits, too, rally round me; I pick up
And use the arms that strewed the ground before,
Unnoticed or spurned aside: I take my stand,
Make my defence. God shall not lose a life
May do Him further service, while I speak
And you hear, you my judges and last hope!
You are the law: 'tis to the law I look.
I began life by hanging to the law,
To the law it is I hang till life shall end.
My brother made appeal to the Pope, 'tis true,
To stay proceedings, judge my cause himself
Nor trouble law,—some fondness of conceit
That rectitude, sagacity sufficed
The investigator in a case like mine,
Dispensed with the machine of law. The Pope
Knew better, set aside my brother's plea
And put me back to law,—referred the cause
Ad judices meos,—doubtlessly did well.
Here, then, I clutch my judges,—I claim law—
Cry, by the higher law whereof your law
O' the land is humbly representative,—
Cry, on what point is it, where either accuse,
I fail to furnish you defence? I stand
Acquitted, actually or virtually,
By every intermediate kind of court
That takes account of right or wrong in man,
Each unit in the series that begins

With God's throne, ends with the tribunal here.
God breathes, not speaks, his verdicts, felt not heard,
Passed on successively to each court I call
Man's conscience, custom, manners, all that make
More and more effort to promulgate, mark
God's verdict in determinable words,
Till last come human jurists—solidify
Fluid result,—what's fixable lies forged,
Statute,—the residue escapes in fume,
Yet hangs aloft, a cloud, as palpable
To the finer sense as word the legist welds.
Justinian's Pandects only make precise
What simply sparkled in men's eyes before,
Twitched in their brow or quivered on their lip,
Waited the speech they called but would not come.
These courts then, whose decree your own confirms,—
Take my whole life, not this last act alone,
Look on it by the light reflected thence!

Walt Whitman (1819–1892)

Thought

Of Justice—as if Justice could be any thing but the same
ample law, expounded by natural judges and saviors,
As if it might be this thing or that thing, according to
decisions.

Walt Whitman (1819–1892)

You Felons on Trial in Courts

You felons on trial in courts,
You convicts in prison-cells, you sentenced assassins chain'd and
handcuff'd with iron,
Who am I too that I am not on trial or in prison?
Me ruthless and devilish as any, that my wrists are not chain'd with iron, or
my ankles with iron?

You prostitutes flaunting over the trottoirs or obscene in your rooms,
Who am I that I should call you more obscene than myself?

O culpable! I acknowledge—I exposé!
(O admirers, praise not me—compliment not me—you make me wince,
I see what you do not—I know what you do not.)

Inside these breast-bones I lie smutch'd and choked,
Beneath this face that appears so impassive hell's tides continually run,
Lusts and wickedness are acceptable to me,
I walk with delinquents with passionate love,
I feel I am of them—I belong to those convicts and prostitutes myself,
And henceforth I will not deny them—for how can I deny myself?

Emily Dickinson (1830–1886)

I Read My Sentence Steadily

I read my sentence—steadily—
Reviewed it with my eyes,
To see that I made no mistake
In its extremest clause—
The Date, and manner, of the shame—
And then the Pious Form
That "God have mercy" on the Soul
The Jury voted Him—
I made my soul familiar—with her extremity—
That at the last, it should not be a novel Agony—
But she, and Death, acquainted—
Meet tranquilly, as friends—
Salute, and pass, without a Hint—
And there, the Matter ends—

Emily Dickinson (1830–1886)

I Had Some Things That I Called Mine

I had some things that I called mine—
And God, that he called his,
Till, recently a rival Claim
Disturbed these amities.

The property, my garden,
Which having sown with care,
He claims the pretty acre,
And sends a Bailiff there.

The station of the parties
Forbids publicity,
But Justice is sublimer
Than arms, or pedigree.

I'll institute an "Action"—
I'll vindicate the law—
Jove! Choose your counsel—
I retain "Shaw"!

Lewis Carroll (1832–1898)

The Barrister's Dream

They sought it with thimbles, they sought it with care;
  They pursued it with forks and hope;
They threatened its life with a railway-share;
  They charmed it with smiles and soap.

But the Barrister, weary of proving in vain
  That the Beaver's lace-making was wrong,
Fell asleep, and in dreams saw the creature quite plain
  That his fancy had dwelt on so long.

He dreamed that he stood in a shadowy Court,
  Where the Snark, with a glass in its eye,
Dressed in gown, bands, and wig, was defending a pig
  On the charge of deserting its sty.

The Witnesses proved, without error or flaw,
  That the sty was deserted when found:
And the Judge kept explaining the state of the law
  In a soft under-current of sound.

The indictment had never been clearly expressed,
  And it seemed that the Snark had begun,
And had spoken three hours, before any one guessed
  What the pig was supposed to have done.

The Jury had each formed a different view
  (Long before the indictment was read),
And they all spoke at once, so that none of them knew
  One word that the others had said.

"You must know—" said the Judge: but the Snark exclaimed, "Fudge!
  That statute is obsolete quite!
Let me tell you, my friends, the whole question depends
  On an ancient manorial right.

"In the matter of Treason the pig would appear
  To have aided, but scarcely abetted:
While the charge of Insolvency fails, it is clear,
  If you grant the plea 'never indebted.'

"The fact of Desertion I will not dispute:
  But its guilt, as I trust, is removed
(So far as relates to the costs of this suit)
  By the Alibi which has been proved.

"My poor client's fate now depends on your votes."
  Here the speaker sat down in his place,
And directed the Judge to refer to his notes
  And briefly to sum up the case.

But the Judge said he never had summed up before;
  So the Snark undertook it instead,
And summed it so well that it came to far more
  Than the Witnesses ever had said!

When the verdict was called for, the Jury declined,
  As the word was so puzzling to spell;
But they ventured to hope that the Snark wouldn't mind
  Undertaking that duty as well.

So the Snark found the verdict, although, as it owned,
  It was spent with the toils of the day:
When it said the word "GUILTY!" the Jury all groaned,
  And some of them fainted away.

Then the Snark pronounced sentence, the Judge being quite
  Too nervous to utter a word:
When it rose to its feet, there was silence like night,
  And the fall of a pin might he heard.

"Transportation for life" was the sentence it gave,
  "And *then* to be fined forty pound."
The Jury all cheered, though the Judge said he feared
  That the phrase was not legally sound.

But their wild exultation was suddenly checked
  When the jailer informed them, with tears,
Such a sentence would have not the slightest effect,
  As the pig had been dead for some years.

The Judge left the Court, looking deeply disgusted:
  But the Snark, though a little aghast,
As the lawyer to whom the defence was intrusted,
  Went bellowing on to the last.

Thus the Barrister dreamed, while the bellowing seemed
  To grow every moment more clear:
Till he woke to the knell of a furious bell,
  Which the Bellman rang close at his ear.

Thomas Hardy (1840–1928)

The Mock Wife

It's a dark drama, this; and yet I know the house, and date;
That is to say, the where and when John Channing met his fate.
The house was one in High Street, seen of burghers still alive,
The year was some two centuries bygone; seventeen-hundred and five.

And dying was Channing the grocer. All the clocks had struck eleven,
And the watchers saw that ere the dawn his soul would be in Heaven;
When he said on a sudden: "I should *like* to kiss her before I go,—
For one last time!" They looked at each other and murmured, "Even so."

She'd just been haled to prison, his wife; yea, charged with shaping his
death:
By poison, 'twas told; and now he was nearing the moment of his last
breath:
He, witless that his young housemate was suspect of such a crime,
Lay thinking that his pangs were but a malady of the time.

Outside the room they pondered gloomily, wondering what to do,
As still he craved her kiss—the dying man who nothing knew:
"Guilty she may not be," they said; "so why should we torture him
In these his last few minutes of life? Yet how indulge his whim?"

And as he begged there piteously for what could not be done,
And the murder-charge had flown about the town to every one,
The friends around him in their trouble thought of a hasty plan,
And straightway set about it. Let denounce them all who can.

"O will you do a kindly deed—it may be a soul to save;
At least, great misery to a man with one foot in the grave?"
Thus they to the buxom woman not unlike his prisoned wife;
"The difference he's past seeing; it will soothe his sinking life."

Well, the friendly neighbour did it; and he kissed her; held her fast;
Kissed her again and yet again. "I—knew she'd—come at last!—
Where have you been?—Ah, kept away!—I'm sorry—overtried—
God bless you!" And he loosed her, fell back tiredly, and died.

His wife stood six months after on the scaffold before the crowd,
Ten thousand of them gathered there; fixed, silent, and hard-browed,
To see her strangled and burnt to dust, as was the verdict then
On women truly judged, or false, of doing to death their men.

Some of them said as they watched her burn: "I am glad he never knew,
Since a few hold her as innocent—think such she could not do!
Glad, too, that (as they tell) he thought she kissed him ere he died."
And they seemed to make no question that the cheat was justified.

Oscar Wilde (1854–1900)

from The Ballad of Reading Gaol

I know not whether Laws be right,
  Or whether Laws be wrong;
All that we know who lie in gaol
  Is that the wall is strong;
And that each day is like a year,
  A year whose days are long.

But this I know, that every Law
  That men have made for Man,
Since first Man took his brother's life,
  And the sad world began,
But straws the wheat and saves the chaff
  With a most evil fan.

This too I know—and wise it were
  If each could know the same—
That every prison that men build
  Is built with bricks of shame,
And bound with bars lest Christ should see
  How men their brothers maim.

With bars they blur the gracious moon,
  And blind the goodly sun:
And they do well to hide their Hell,
  For in it things are done
That Son of God nor son of Man
  Ever should look upon!

A. E. Housman (1859–1936)

Oh Who Is That Young Sinner

Oh who is that young sinner with the handcuffs on his wrists?
And what has he been after that they groan and shake their fists?
And wherefore is he wearing such a conscience-stricken air?
Oh they're taking him to prison for the color of his hair.

'Tis a shame to human nature, such a head of hair as his;
In the good old time 'twas hanging for the color that it is;
Though hanging isn't bad enough and flaying would be fair
For the nameless and abominable color of his hair.

Oh a deal of pains he's taken and a pretty price he's paid
To hide his poll or dye it of a mentionable shade;
But they've pulled the beggar's hat off for the world to see and stare,
And they're taking him to justice for the color of his hair.

Now 'tis oakum for his fingers and the treadmill for his feet,
And the quarry-gang on Portland in the cold and in the heat,
And between his spells of labor in the time he has to spare
He can curse the God that made him for the color of his hair.

Rudyard Kipling (1865–1936)

The Reeds of Runnymede

(Magna Charta, June 15, 1215)

At Runnymede, at Runnymede,
What say the reeds at Runnymede?
The lissom reeds that give and take,
That bend so far, but never break.
They keep the sleepy Thames awake
With tales of John at Runnymede.

At Runnymede, at Runnymede,
Oh, hear the reeds at Runnymede:—
"You mustn't sell, delay, deny,
A freeman's right or liberty.
It wakes the stubborn Englishry,
We saw 'em roused at Runnymede!

"When through our ranks the Barons came,
With little thought of praise or blame,
But resolute to play the game,
They lumbered up to Runnymede;
And there they launched in solid line
The first attack on Right Divine—
The curt, uncompromising "Sign!"
That settled John at Runnymede.

"At Runnymede, at Runnymede,
Your rights were won at Runnymede!
No freeman shall be fined or bound,
Or dispossessed of freehold ground,
Except by lawful judgment found

And passed upon him by his peers.
Forget not, after all these years,
  The Charter signed at Runnymede."

And still when Mob or Monarch lays
Too rude a hand on English ways,
The whisper wakes, the shudder plays,
  Across the reeds at Runnymede.
And Thames, that knows the moods of kings,
And crowds and priests and suchlike things,
Rolls deep and dreadful as he brings
  Their warning down from Runnymede!

Edgar Lee Masters (1868–1950)

"Butch" Weldy

After I got religion and steadied down
They gave me a job in the canning works,
And every morning I had to fill
The tank in the yard with gasoline,
That fed the blow-fires in the sheds
To heat the soldering irons.
And I mounted a rickety ladder to do it,
Carrying buckets full of the stuff.
One morning, as I stood there pouring,
The air grew still and seemed to heave,
And I shot up as the tank exploded,
And down I came with both legs broken,
And my eyes burned crisp as a couple of eggs
For someone left a blow-fire going,
And something sucked the flame in the tank.
The Circuit Judge said whoever did it
Was a fellow-servant of mine, and so
Old Rhodes' son didn't have to pay me.
And I sat on the witness stand as blind
As Jack the Fiddler, saying over and over,
"I didn't know him at all."

Edgar Lee Masters (1868–1950)

Judge Selah Lively

Suppose you stood just five feet two,
And had worked your way as a grocery clerk,
Studying law by candle light
Until you became an attorney at law?
And then suppose through your diligence,
And regular church attendance,
You became attorney for Thomas Rhodes,
Collecting notes and mortgages,
And representing all the widows
In the Probate Court? And through it all
They jeered at your size, and laughed at your clothes
And your polished boots? And then suppose
You became the County Judge?
And Jefferson Howard and Kinsey Keene,
And Harmon Whitney, and all the giants
Who had sneered at you, were forced to stand
Before the bar and say "Your Honor"—
Well, don't you think it was natural
That I made it hard for them?

Edgar Lee Masters (1868–1950)

State's Attorney Fallas

I, the scourge-wielder, balance-wrecker,
Smiter with whips and swords;
I, hater of the breakers of the law;
I, legalist, inexorable and bitter,
Driving the jury to hang the madman, Barry Holden,
Was made as one dead by light too bright for eyes,
And woke to face a Truth with bloody brow:
Steel forceps fumbled by a doctor's hand
Against my boy's head as he entered life
Made him an idiot.
I turned to books of science
To care for him.
That's how the world of those whose minds are sick
Became my work in life, and all my world.
Poor ruined boy! You were, at last, the potter
And I and all my deeds of charity
The vessels of your hand.

Edgar Lee Masters (1868–1950)

Carl Hamblin

The press of the Spoon River *Clarion* was wrecked,
And I was tarred and feathered,
For publishing this on the day the Anarchists were hanged in Chicago:
"I saw a beautiful woman with bandaged eyes
Standing on the steps of a marble temple.
Great multitudes passed in front of her,
Lifting their faces to her imploringly.
In her left hand she held a sword.
She was brandishing the sword,
Sometimes striking a child, again a laborer,
Again a slinking woman, again a lunatic.
In her right hand she held a scale;
Into the scale pieces of gold were tossed
By those who dodged the strokes of the sword.
A man in a black gown read from a manuscript:
'She is no respecter of persons.'
Then a youth wearing a red cap
Leaped to her side and snatched away the bandage.
And lo, the lashes had been eaten away
From the oozy eye-lids;
The eye-balls were seared with a milky mucus;
The madness of a dying soul
Was written on her face—
But the multitude saw why she wore the bandage."

W. H. Davies (1871–1940)

The Inquest

I took my oath I would inquire,
  Without affection, hate, or wrath,
Into the death of Ada Wright—
  So help me God! I took that oath.

When I went out to see the corpse,
  The four months' babe that died so young,
I judged it was seven pounds in weight,
  And little more than one foot long.

One eye, that had a yellow lid,
  Was shut—so was the mouth, that smiled;
The left eye open, shining bright—
  It seemed a knowing little child.

For as I looked at that one eye,
  It seemed to laugh, and say with glee:
"What caused my death you'll never know—
  Perhaps my mother murdered me."

When I went into court again
  To hear the mother's evidence—
It was a love-child, she explained.
  And smiled, for our intelligence.

"Now, Gentlemen of the Jury," said
  The coroner—"this woman's child
By misadventure met its death."
  "Aye, aye," said we. The mother smiled.

And I could see that child's one eye
  Which seemed to laugh, and say with glee:
"What caused my death you'll never know—
  Perhaps my mother murdered me."

Walter de la Mare (1873–1956)

In the Dock

Pallid, mis-shapen he stands. The World's grimed thumb,
Now hooked securely in his matted hair,
Has haled him struggling from his poisonous slum
And flung him, mute as fish, close-netted there.
His bloodless hands entalon that iron rail.
He gloats in beastlike trance. His settling eyes
From staring face to face rove on—and quail.
Justice for carrion pants; and these the flies.
Voice after voice in smooth impartial drone
Erects horrific in his darkening brain
A timber framework, where agape, alone
Bright life will kiss good-bye the cheek of Cain.
Sudden like wolf he cries; and sweats to see
When howls man's soul, it howls inaudibly.

Carl Sandburg (1878–1967)

The Lawyers Know Too Much

The lawyers, Bob, know too much.
They are chums of the books of old John Marshall.
They know it all, what a dead hand wrote,
A stiff dead hand and its knuckles crumbling,
The bones of the fingers a thin white ash.
        The lawyers know
        a dead man's thoughts too well.

In the heels of the higgling lawyers, Bob,
Too many slippery ifs and buts and howevers,
Too much hereinbefore provided whereas,
Too many doors to go in and out of.

        When the lawyers are through
        What is there left, Bob?
        Can a mouse nibble at it
        And find enough to fasten a tooth in?

        Why is there always a secret singing
        When a lawyer cashes in?
        Why does a hearse horse snicker
        Hauling a lawyer away?

The work of a bricklayer goes to the blue.
The knack of a mason outlasts a moon.
The hands of a plasterer hold a room together.
The land of a farmer wishes him back again.
        Singers of songs and dreamers of plays
        Build a house no wind blows over.
The lawyers—tell me why a hearse horse snickers hauling a lawyer's bones.

William Carlos Williams (1883–1963)

Impromptu: The Suckers

Take it out in vile whisky, take it out
in lifting your skirts to show your silken
crotches; it is this that is intended.
You are it. Your pleas will always be denied.
You too will always go up with the two guys,
scapegoats to save the Republic and
especially the State of Massachusetts. The
Governor says so and you ain't supposed
to ask for details—

Your case has been reviewed by high-minded
and unprejudiced observers (like hell
they were!) the president of a great
university, the president of a noteworthy
technical school and a judge too old to sit
on the bench, men already rewarded for
their services to pedagogy and the enforcement
of arbitrary statutes. In other words
pimps to tradition—

Why in hell didn't they choose some other
kind of "unprejudiced adviser" for their
death council? instead of sticking to that
autocratic strain of Boston backwash, except
that the council was far from unprejudiced
but the product of a rejected, discredited
class long since outgrown except for use in
courts and school, and that they
wanted it so—

Why didn't they choose at least one decent
Jew or some fair-minded Negro or anybody
but such a triumvirate of inversion, the
New England aristocracy, bent on working off
a grudge against you, Americans, you
are the suckers, you are the ones who will
be going up on the eleventh to get the current
shot into you, for the glory of the state
and the perpetuation of abstract justice—

And all this in the face of the facts: that
the man who swore, and deceived the jury
wilfully by so doing, that the bullets found
in the bodies of the deceased could be
identified as having been fired from the pistol
of one of the accused—later
acknowledged that he could not so identify
them; that the jurors now seven years after
the crime do not remember the details and
have wanted to forget them; that the
prosecution has never succeeded in
apprehending the accomplices nor in connecting
the prisoners with any of the loot stolen—

The case is perfect against you, all the
documents say so—in spite of the fact that
it is reasonably certain that you were not
at the scene of the crime, shown, quite as
convincingly as the accusing facts in the
court evidence, by better reasoning to have
been committed by someone else with whom
the loot can be connected and among whom the
accomplices can be found—

It's no use, you are Americans, just the dregs.
It's all you deserve. You've got the cash,

what the hell do you care? You've got
nothing to lose. You are inheritors of a great
tradition. My country right or wrong!
You do what you're told to do. You don't
answer back the way Tommy Jeff did or Ben
Frank or Georgie Washing. I'll say you
don't. You're civilized. You let your
betters tell you where you get off. Go
ahead—

But after all, the thing that swung heaviest
against you was that you were scared when
they copped you. Explain that you
nature's nobleman! For you know that every
American is innocent and at peace in his
own heart. He hasn't a damned thing to be
afraid of. He knows the government is for
him. Why, when a cop steps up and grabs
you at night you just laugh and think it's
a hell of a good joke—

This is what was intended from the first.
So take it out in your rotten whisky and
silk underwear. That's what *you* get out of
it. But put it down in your memory that this
is the kind of stuff that they can't get away
with. It is there and it's loaded. No one
can understand what makes the present age
what it is. They are mystified by certain
insistences.

D. H. Lawrence (1885–1930)

Auto-da-Fé

Help! Help! they want to burn my pictures,
they want to make an *auto-da-fé*!
They want to make an *act of faith,* and burn my pretty pictures.
They've seized them and carried them away!

Help! Help! I am calling still in English;
is the language dead and empty of reply!
An Unholy Inquisition has arrested all my pictures,
a magistrate, and six fat smaller fry.

Six fat smaller bobbies are the inquisitors minor
who've decided that Boccaccio must burn.
But the Grand Inquisitor is a stale old magistrate
in Marlborough Road, and it is now his turn.

Oh he has put his pince-nez on, and stoutly has stepped down
to the police-station cell
where my darling pictures, prisoners, await his deadly frown
and his grand-inquisitorial knell.

Oh he knows all about it, he casts a yellow eye
on the gardener whose shirt's blown back:
Burn that!—he sees Eve running from the likes of him: I
order you, destroy the whole vile pack.

All my pretty pictures huddled in the dark awaiting
their doom at the hands of Mr. Meade.
But the day they burn my pictures they burn the rose of England
and fertilize the weeds on every mead.

Help! Oh help! they want to burn my pictures:
we've got the Inquisition back
with a set of cankered magistrates and busy-busy bobbies.
Look out, my lad, you've got 'em on your track.

Edna St. Vincent Millay (1892–1950)

Justice Denied in Massachusetts

Let us abandon then our gardens and go home
And sit in the sitting-room.
Shall the larkspur blossom or the corn grow under this cloud?
Sour to the fruitful seed
Is the cold earth under this cloud,
Fostering quack and weed, we have marched upon but cannot conquer;
We have bent the blades of our hoes against the stalks of them.

Let us go home, and sit in the sitting-room.
Not in our day
Shall the cloud go over and the sun rise as before,
Beneficent upon us
Out of the glittering bay,
And the warm winds be blown inward from the sea
Moving the blades of corn
With a peaceful sound.
Forlorn, forlorn,
Stands the blue hay-rack by the empty mow.
And the petals drop to the ground,
Leaving the tree unfruited.
The sun that warmed our stooping backs and withered the weed
   uprooted—
We shall not feel it again.
We shall die in darkness, and be buried in the rain.

What from the splendid dead
We have inherited—
Furrows sweet to the grain, and the weed subdued—
See now the slug and the mildew plunder.
Evil does overwhelm

The larkspur and the corn;
We have seen them go under.

Let us sit here, sit still,
Here in the sitting-room until we die;
At the step of Death on the walk, rise and go;
Leaving to our children's children this beautiful doorway,
And this elm,
And a blighted earth to till
With a broken hoe.

Charles Reznikoff (1894–1976)

from "Early History of a Writer"

I now went to law school in the evening.
The instruction was by reading cases—
no lectures that stuffed pap into the mouth of the student;
and we soon learned, under the incitement of our teachers,
to question—if questioning was called for—
the opinion of each case
and, perhaps, that of our teachers.
Most of my fellow students were older than I
and earnest (almost all worked during the day
in factories or in law offices),
and their questions had steel in them;
unlike the students in the morning or afternoon classes,
mostly just out of high school
and too timid to speak or, if they did,
poked feeble questions
like the sticks that children use as swords.
At first I read more poetry than cases,
but then threw myself zestfully
into the dog fight that each period became
and, to be ready for it,
learned to probe beneath the facts of each case
for the living principle of law
and to trace it, if I could,
to the solid trunk from which it sprang;
confused as it all was to me at first,
I soon saw the law in its elements as a beautiful order
in which benefit balanced obligation
and nothing was without its reason—or reasons.

The law that we studied
was not always the actual law

of judges or statutes
but an ideal—
from which new branches were ever springing
as society became complicated
and the new rights of its individuals clear.
I found it delightful
to climb those green heights,
to bathe in the clear waters of reason,
to use words for their daylight meaning
and not as prisms
playing with the rainbows of connotation:
after the dim lights, the colored phrases, the cloying music,
the hints of what the poets meant
and did not quite say
(for to suggest was to create
and to name was to destroy—
according to the Symbolists, at least),
the plain sunlight of the cases,
the sharp prose,
the forthright speech of the judges;
it was good, too, to stick my mind against the sentences of a judge,
and drag the meaning out of the shell of words.
And when our teacher of contracts,
who was also the dean of the school,
produced a theory of acceptance
(which was not actually the law anywhere),
I was delighted, walking along the streets deep in thought,
to find a flaw in the theory
and boldly produce another, my very own—
to find that I, too, could think like a lawyer.

I soon had no time for writing or reading anything but law
and spent my days in the law library
diligently reading cases and memorizing sentences that seemed meaty;
reading each page as often as I liked
with nothing to jog my elbow or step on my heel;

sifting the facts of each case until I had only the hard essentials;
underlining words and phrases
until I had plotted the judge's reasoning;
and digging for the bedrock of law on which the cases stood—
or did not stand.
The noise of the street was far away—
ten storeys below;
far away, too, the worry and noise of my parents' shop;
before me was all that was left of eager argument and eager parties,
now merely names that might just as well have been,
and in the talk of the law students often were,
single letters of the alphabet:
all the blood—the heartache and the heartening—gone out of the words
and only, as a pattern for thinking,
the cool bones of the judge's reasoning.
And I felt no regret for the glittering words I had played with
and only pleasure to be working with ideas—
of rights and wrongs and their elements
and of justice between men in their intricate affairs.

The last class was over at ten.
I would try to get home before midnight
and had to walk briskly to do it:
a mile or two to the bridge
through streets now mostly empty and still;
over the bridge again,
often meeting with nobody for the whole mile of it,
especially if the wind was cold or when it would snow or rain;
and then the long walk in Brooklyn, five or six miles,
the streets quiet and dark and the neighborhood of my home
quietest of all—
lawns and gardens, a park and empty lots.

Suddenly all delight in my studies was gone—
melted with the snow in the spring.
True enough, the studies of the second year were less interesting

than those of the first:
less probing after principle and more of practice,
less general reasoning and more of statutory requirement,
necessary enough but detailed and dull;
but what bothered me most, unlooked for
and against will and reason,
with the suddenness of a fever,
was the longing to write:
as if all that I had seen and heard and remembered
and, for the most part, felt only slightly,
was not gone, as I had thought,
but stored in a reservoir
that now, filled to the brim, was overrunning—
pouring over on all sides.
(It was, of course, no reservoir, but only a kettleful—
but it had come to a boil.)
And here I was, busied with this tiresome study of the law,
these tiring studies that left me no time
and, if time, no strength
to write. My bulky lawbooks had become, over night,
too heavy to lift and the cases palaver.

Stephen Vincent Benét (1898–1943)

from John Brown's Body

On Saturday, in Southern market towns,
When I was a boy with twenty cents to spend,
The carts began to drift in with the morning,
And, by the afternoon, the slipshod Square
And all broad Center Street were lined with them;
Moth-eaten mules that whickered at each other
Between the mended shafts of rattletrap wagons,
Mud-spattered buggies, mouldy phaetons,
And, here and there, an ox-cart from the hills
Whose solemn team had shoulders of rough, white rock,
Innocent noses, black and wet as snailshells,
And that inordinate patience in their eyes.

There always was a Courthouse in the Square,
A cupolaed Courthouse, drowsing Time away
Behind the grey-white pillars of its porch
Like an old sleepy judge in a spotted gown;
And, down the Square, always a languid jail
Of worn, uneven brick with moss in the cracks
Or stone weathered the grey of weathered pine.
The plump jail-master wore a linen duster
In summer, and you used to see him sit
Tilted against the wall in a pine-chair,
Spitting reflectively in the warm dust
While endless afternoons slowly dissolved
Into the longer shadow, the dust-blue twilight.
Higgledy-piggledy days—days that are gone—
The trotters are dead, all the yellow-painted sulkies
Broken for firewood—the old Courthouse grins
Through new false-teeth of Alabama limestone—
The haircloth lap-robe weeps on a Ford radiator—

But I have seen the old Courthouse. I have seen
The flyspecked windows and the faded flag
Over the judge's chair, touched the scuffed walls,
Spat in the monumental brass spittoons
And smelt the smell that never could be aired,
Although one opened windows for a year,
The unforgettable, intangible
Mixture of cheap cigars, worm-eaten books,
Sweat, poverty, negro hair-oil, grief and law.
I have seen the long room packed with quiet men,
Fit to turn mob, if need were, in a flash—
Cocked-pistol men, so lazily attentive
Their easy languor knocked against your ribs
As, hour by hour, the lawyers droned along,
And minute on creeping minute, your cold necknape
Waited the bursting of the firecracker,
The flare of fury.

And yet, that composed fury
Burnt itself out, unflaring—was held down
By a dry, droning voice, a faded flag.
The kettle never boiled, the pistol stayed
At cock but the snake-head hammer never fell. . . .
The little boys climbed down beyond the windows. . . .

So, in the cupolaed Courthouse there in Charlestown,
When the jail-guards had carried in the cot
Where Brown lay like a hawk with a broken back,
I hear the rustle of the moving crowd,
The buzz outside, taste the dull, heavy air,
Smell the stale smell and see the country carts
Hitched in the streets.

For a long, dragging week
Of market-Saturdays the trial went on.
The droning voices rise and fall and rise.
Stevens lies quiet on his mattress, breathing
The harsh and difficult breath of a dying man,

Although not dying then.

Beyond the Square

The trees are dry, but all the dry leaves not fallen—
Yellow leaves falling through a grey-blue dusk,
The first winds of November whirl and scatter them. . . .

Read as you will in any of the books,
The details of the thing, the questions and answers,
How sometimes Brown would walk, sometimes was carried,
At first would hardly plead, half-refused counsel,
Accepted later, made up witness-lists,
Grew fitfully absorbed in his defense,
Only to flare in temper at his first lawyers
And drive them from the case.

Questions and answers,

Wheels creaking in a void.

Sometimes he lay

Quiet upon his cot, the hawk-eyes staring.
Sometimes his fingers moved mechanically
As if at their old task of sorting wool,
Fingertips that could tell him in the dark
Whether the wool they touched was from Ohio
Or from Vermont. They had the shepherd's gift.
It was his one sure talent.

Questions creaking

Uselessly back and forth.

No one can say

That the trial was not fair. The trial was fair,
Painfully fair by every rule of law,
And that it was made not the slightest difference.
The law's our yardstick, and it measures well
Or well enough when there are yards to measure.
Measure a wave with it, measure a fire,
Cut sorrow up in inches, weigh content.
You can weigh John Brown's body well enough,
But how and in what balance weigh John Brown?

He had the shepherd's gift, but that was all.
He had no other single gift for life.
Some men are pasture Death turns back to pasture,
Some are fire-opals on that iron wrist,
Some the deep roots of wisdoms not yet born.
John Brown was none of these,
He was a stone,
A stone eroded to a cutting edge
By obstinacy, failure and cold prayers.
Discredited farmer, dubiously involved
In lawsuit after lawsuit, Shubel Morgan
Fantastic bandit of the Kansas border,
Red-handed murderer at Pottawattomie,
Cloudy apostle, whooped along to death
By those who do no violence themselves
But only buy the guns to have it done,
Sincere of course, as all fanatics are,
And with a certain minor-prophet air,
That fooled the world to thinking him half-great
When all he did consistently was fail.
So far one advocate.

But there is this.

Sometimes there comes a crack in Time itself.
Sometimes the earth is torn by something blind.
Sometimes an image that has stood so long
It seems implanted as the polar star
Is moved against an unfathomed force
That suddenly will not have it any more.
Call it the *mores,* call it God or Fate,
Call it Mansoul or economic law,
That force exists and moves.

And when it moves
It will employ a hard and actual stone
To batter into bits an actual wall

And change the actual scheme of things.
John Brown
Was such a stone—unreasoning as the stone,
Destructive as the stone, and, if you like,
Heroic and devoted as such a stone.
He had no gift for life, no gift to bring
Life but his body and a cutting edge,
But he knew how to die.
And yardstick law
Gave him six weeks to burn that hoarded knowledge
In one swift fire whose sparks fell like live coals
On every State in the Union.
Listen now,
Listen, the bearded lips are speaking now,
There are no more guerilla-raids to plan,
There are no more hard questions to be solved
Of right and wrong, no need to beg for peace,
Here is the peace unbegged, here is the end,
Here is the insolence of the sun cast off,
Here is the voice already fixed with night.

JOHN BROWN'S SPEECH

I have, may it please the Court, a few words to say.

In the first place I deny everything but what I have all along admitted: of a design on my part to free slaves. . . .

Had I interfered in the matter which I admit, and which I admit has been fairly proved . . . had I so interfered in behalf of the rich, the powerful, the intelligent, or the so-called great . . . and suffered and sacrificed, what I have in this interference, it would have been all right. Every man in this Court would have deemed it an act worthy of reward rather than punishment.

I see a book kissed which I suppose to be the Bible, or at least the New Testament, which teaches me that all things whatsoever I would that men should do unto me, I should do even so to them. It teaches me further to remember them that are in bonds as bound with them. I endeavored to act up to that instruction. I say I am yet too young to understand that God is any respecter of persons. I believe that to have interfered as I have done, as I have always freely admitted I have done in behalf of His despised poor, I did no wrong, but right. Now, if it is deemed necessary that I should forfeit my life for the furtherance of the ends of justice and mingle my blood further with the blood of my children and with the blood of millions in this slave country whose rights are disregarded by wicked, cruel and unjust enactments, I say, let it be done.

Let me say one word further. I feel entirely satisfied with the treatment I have received on my trial. Considering all the circumstances, it has been more generous than I expected. But I feel no consciousness of guilt. I have stated from the first what was my intention and what was not. I never had any design against the liberty of any person, nor any disposition to commit treason or incite slaves to rebel or make any general insurrection. I never encouraged any man to do so but always discouraged any idea of that kind.

Let me say also, in regard to the statements made by some of those connected with me, I hear it has been stated by some of them that I have induced them to join with me. But the contrary is true. I do not say this to injure them, but as regretting their weakness. Not one but joined me of his own accord, and the greater part at their own expense. A number of them I never saw, and never had a word of conversation with, till the day they came to me, and that was for the purpose I have stated.

Now I have done.

The voice ceased. There was a deep, brief pause.
The judge pronounced the formal words of death.
One man, a stranger, tried to clap his hands.
The foolish sound was stopped.
There was nothing but silence then.
                                        No cries in the court,
No roar, no slightest murmur from the thronged street,
As Brown went back to jail between his guards.
The heavy door shut behind them.
There was a noise of chairs scraped back in the court-room,
And that huge sigh of a crowd turning back into men.

Yvor Winters (1900–1968)

To Edwin V. McKenzie

On his defense of David Lamson

The concept lives, but few men fill the frame;
Greatness is difficult: the certain aim,
The powerful body, and the nervous skill,
The acquiring mind, and the untiring will,
The just man's fury and uplifted arm,
And the strong heart, to keep the weak from harm.
This is the great man of tradition, one
To point out justice when the wrong is done;
To outwit rogue and craven; represent
Mankind in the eternal sacrament—
Odysseus, with the giant weapon bent.

When those who guard tradition in the schools
Proved to be weaklings and half-learnëd fools,
You took the burden, saved the intellect.
Combating treason, mastering each defect,
You fought your battle, inch by inch of ground.
When Justice had become an angry sound,
When Judgment dwindled to an angry man,
You named the limits of the civil span:
I saw you, mantled in tradition, tower;
You filled the courtroom with historic power;
Yourself the concept in the final hour.

Kenneth Fearing (1902–1961)

The People v. The People

I have never seen him, this invisible member of the panel, this thirteenth juror, but I have certain clues;
I know, after so many years of practice, though I cannot prove I know;
It is enough to say, I know that I know.

He is five feet nine or ten, with piercing, bright, triumphant eyes;
He needs glasses, which he will not wear, and he is almost certainly stone deaf.
(Cf. Blair v. Gregg, which he utterly ruined.)
He is the juror forever looking out of the window, secretly smiling, when you make your telling point.
The one who is wide awake when you think he is asleep. The man who naps with his eyes wide open.
Those same triumphant eyes.
He is the man who knows. And knows that he knows.

His hair is meager and he wears wash ties, but these are not important points.
He likes the legal atmosphere, that is plain, because he is always there.
It is the decent, the orderly procedure that he likes.
He is the juror who arrived first, though you thought he was late; the one who failed to return from lunch, though you had not noticed.

Let me put it like this: He is the cause of your vague uneasiness when you glance about and see that the other twelve are all right.

I would know him if I were to see him, I could swear to his identity, if I actually saw him once;
I nearly overheard him when I was for the defense: "They never indict anyone unless they are guilty";

And when I was the State: "A poor man (or a rich man) doesn't stand a
chance."
Always, before the trial's end, he wants to know if the sergeant knew the
moon was full on that particular night.

And none of this matters, except I am convinced he is the unseen juror
bribed, bought, and planted by The People,
An enemy of reason and precedent, a friend of illogic,
Something, I now know, that I know that I really know—

And he or anyone else is welcome to my Blackstone, or my crowded
shelves of standard books,
In exchange for the monumental works I am convinced he has been
writing through the years:
"The Rules of Hearsay"; "The Laws of Rumor";
"An Omnibus Guide to Chance and Superstition," by One Who Knows.

Langston Hughes (1902–1967)

The Town of Scottsboro

Scottsboro's just a little place:
No shame is writ across its face—
Its court, too weak to stand against a mob,
Its people's heart, too small to hold a sob.

William Empson (1906–1984)

Legal Fiction

Law makes long spokes of the short stakes of men.
Your well fenced out real estate of mind
No high flat of the nomad citizen
Looks over, or train leaves behind.

Your rights extend under and above your claim
Without bound; you own land in Heaven and Hell;
Your part of earth's surface and mass the same,
Of all cosmos' volume, and all stars as well.

Your rights reach down where all owners meet, in Hell's
Pointed exclusive conclave, at earth's center
(Your spun farm's root still on that axis dwells);
And up, through galaxies, a growing sector.

You are nomad yet; the lighthouse beam you own
Flashes, like Lucifer, through the firmament.
Earth's axis varies; your dark central cone
Wavers a candle's shadow, at the end.

W. H. Auden (1907–1973)

Law Like Love

Law, say the gardeners, is the sun,
Law is the one
All gardeners obey
To-morrow, yesterday, to-day.

Law is the wisdom of the old,
The impotent grandfathers feebly scold;
The grandchildren put out a treble tongue,
Law is the senses of the young.

Law, says the priest with a priestly look,
Expounding to an unpriestly people,
Law is the words in my priestly book,
Law is my pulpit and my steeple.
Law, says the judge as he looks down his nose,
Speaking clearly and most severely,
Law is as I've told you before,
Law is as you know I suppose,
Law is but let me explain it once more,
Law is The Law.

Yet law-abiding scholars write:
Law is neither wrong nor right,
Law is only crimes
Punished by places and by times,
Law is the clothes men wear
Anytime, anywhere,
Law is Good morning and Good night.

Others say, Law is our Fate;
Others say, Law is our State;

Others say, others say
Law is no more,
Law has gone away.

And always the loud angry crowd,
Very angry and very loud,
Law is We,
And always the soft idiot softly Me.

If we, dear, know we know no more
Than they about the Law,
If I no more than you
Know what we should and should not do
Except that all agree
Gladly or miserably
That the Law is
And that all know this,
If therefore thinking it absurd
To identify Law with some other word,
Unlike so many men
I cannot say Law is again,
No more than they can we suppress
The universal wish to guess
Or slip out of our own position
Into an unconcerned condition.
Although I can at least confine
Your vanity and mine
To stating timidly
A timid similarity,
We shall boast anyway:
Like love I say.

Like love we don't know where or why,
Like love we can't compel or fly,
Like love we often weep,
Like love we seldom keep.

J. V. Cunningham (1911–1985)

The Judge Is Fury

These the assizes: here the charge, denial,
Proof and disproof: the poem is the trial.
Experience is defendant, and the jury
Peers of tradition, and the judge is fury.

Roy Fuller (1912–1991)

The Verdict

The verdict has already been arrived
At. But the foreman of the jury still
Must write the record down laboriously;

And others of the panel go and pee
Or phone to say they will be home for tea,
Before all shamble back into the Court

And the judge summoned from his crossword puzzle.
So that some time goes by before his fate
Can possibly be learnt by the accused.

And more: this was arrived at earlier still—
Before the charge was laid, the jury called,
The trial started. To the prisoner

It comes as no surprise to find himself
Condemned to death. The circumstances merely
(Though often attempted to be conjured up)

Strike him as somewhat odd or poignant. Who
Could have foretold that he would be cut off
During a visit from his fleeting Muse;

Or that he'd be less anguished than embarrassed;
Feel more for his survivors than himself;
Making some verses out of hopeless dread

Of rather more than average tedium?

Muriel Rukeyser (1913–1980)

The Trial

The South is green with coming spring: revival
flourishes in the fields of Alabama. Spongy with rain,
plantations breathe April—carwheels suck mud in the roads,
the town expands warm in the afternoons. At night, the black boy
teeters no-handed on a bicycle, whistling the St. Louis Blues,
blood beating, and hot South. A red brick courthouse
is vicious with men inviting death. Array your judges, call your jurors;
 come,
here is your justice, come out of the crazy jail.
Grass is green now in Alabama; Birmingham dusks are quiet
relaxed and soft in the parks, stern at the yards:
a hundred boxcars shunted off to sidings, and the hoboes
fathering grains of sleep in forbidden corners.
In all the yards: Atlanta, Chattanooga,
Memphis, and New Orleans, the cars, and no jobs.

Every night the mail-planes burrow the sky
carrying postcards to laughing girls in Texas,
passionate letters to the Charleston virgins,
words through the South—and no reprieve,
no pardon, no release.

A blinded statue attends before the courthouse,
bronze and black men lie on the grass, waiting,
the khaki dapper National Guard leans on its bayonets.
But the air is populous beyond our vision:
all the people's anger finds its vortex here
as the mythic lips of justice open, and speak.

Hammers and sickles are carried in a wave of strength, fire-tipped,
swinging passionately ninefold to a shore.

Answer the back-thrown Negro face of the lynched, the flat forehead
    knotted,
the eyes showing a wild iris, the mouth a welter of blood,
answer the broken shoulder and these twisted arms.
John Brown, Nat Turner, Toussaint stand in this courtroom,
Dred Scott wrestles for freedom there in the dark corner,
all our celebrated shambles are repeated here: now again
Sacco and Vanzetti walk to a chair, to the straps and rivets
and the switch spitting death and Massachusetts' will.
Wreaths are brought out of history

here are the well-nourished flowers of France,

grown strong on blood,

Caesar twisting his thin throat toward conquest,

turning north from the Roman laurels,

the Istrian galleys slide again to sea.
How they waded through bloody Godfrey's Jerusalem,
How the fires broke through Europe, and the rich
and the tall jails battened on revolution!
The fastidious Louis', cousins to the sun, stamping
those ribboned heels on Calas, on the people;
the lynched five thousand of America.
Tom Mooney from San Quentin, Herndon: here
is an army for audience

all resolved

to a gibbet of tobacco, spat, and the empanelled hundred,
a jury of vengeance, the cheap pressed lips, the eyes like hardware;
the judge, his eye-sockets and cheeks dark and immutably secret,
the twisting mouth of the prosecuting attorney.
Nine dark boys spread their breasts against Alabama,
schooled in the cells, fathered by want

Mother—one writes—they treat us bad. If they send us
back to Kilby jail, I think I shall kill myself.
I think I must hang myself by my overalls.

Alabama and the South are soft with spring:
in the North the seasons change, sweet April, December and the air
loaded with snow. There is time for meetings
during the years, they remaining in prison.

In the Square

a crowd listens carrying banners.

Overhead, boring through the speaker's voice, a plane
circles with a snoring of motors revolving in the sky
drowning the single voice. It does not touch
the crowd's silence. It circles. The name stands:
Scottsboro.

Dylan Thomas (1914–1953)

The Hand That Signed the Paper

The hand that signed the paper felled a city;
Five sovereign fingers taxed the breath,
Doubled the globe of dead and halved a country;
These five kings did a king to death.

The mighty hand leads to a sloping shoulder,
The finger joints are cramped with chalk;
A goose's quill has put an end to murder
That put an end to talk.

The hand that signed the treaty bred a fever,
And famine grew, and locusts came;
Great is the hand that holds dominion over
Man by a scribbled name.

The five kings count the dead but do not soften
The crusted wound nor stroke the brow;
A hand rules pity as a hand rules heaven;
Hands have no tears to flow.

John Berryman (1914–1972)

Dreamsong 86

The conclusion is growing . . . I feel sure, my lord,
this august court will entertain the plea
Not Guilty by reason of death.
I can say no more except that for the record
I add that all the crimes since all the times he
died will be due to the breath

of unknown others, sweating in their guilt
while my client Henry's brow of stainless steel
rests free, as well it may,
of all such turbulence, whereof not built
Henry lies clear as any onion-peel
in any sandwich, say.

He spiced us: there, my lord, the wicked fault
lodges: we judged him when we did not know
and we did judge him wrong,
lying incapable of crime save salt
preservative in cases here below
adduced. Not to prolong

Weldon Kees (1914–1955)

After the Trial

Hearing the judges' well-considered sentence,
The prisoner saw long plateaus of guilt,
And thought of all the dismal furnished rooms
The past assembled, the eyes of parents
Staring through walls as though forever
To condemn and wound his innocence.

And if I raise my voice, protest my innocence,
The judges won't revoke their sentence.
I could stand screaming in this box forever,
Leaving them deaf to everything but guilt;
All the machinery of law devised by parents
Could not be stopped though fire swept the rooms.

Whenever my thoughts move to all those rooms
I sat alone in, capable of innocence,
I know now I was not alone, that parents
Always were there to speak the hideous sentence:
"You are our son; be good; we know your guilt;
We stare through walls and see your thoughts forever."

Sometimes I wished to go away forever;
I dreamt of strangers and of stranger rooms
Where every corner held the light of guilt.
Why do the judges stare? I saw no innocence
In them when they pronounced the sentence;
I heard instead the believing voice of parents.

I can remember evenings when my parents,
Settling my future happily forever,
Would frown before they spoke the sentence:

"Someday the time will come to leave these rooms
Where, under our watchful eyes, you have been innocent;
Remember us before you seize the world of guilt."

Their eyes burn. How can I deny my guilt
When I am guilty in the sight of parents?
I cannot think that even they were innocent.
At least I shall not have to wait forever
To be escorted to the silent rooms
Where darkness promises a final sentence.

We walk forever to the doors of guilt,
Pursued by our own sentences and eyes of parents,
Never to enter innocent and quiet rooms.

David Ignatow (1914–1997)

The Law Has Reasons

because roads lead to towns
and do not generally end up in marshes
or deserts and because there are men
in session. Each morning they comb their hair
before the glass that shows the fine vapor
of their existence; they sit in chambers
for its exact word, neither sullen
nor filled with despair: dust too
must be as dust underfoot or on table
each morning wiped with a cloth clean.

John Ciardi (1916–1986)

E Is for Earwig

Earwigs are not
imaginary in themselves but imagined
to be more than they are. There is
some such beastlet in every codification,
Law itself being made not of realities
but of secularized mythology.

Legally classified *Forficulida* and distinguishable
by its wing structure and its tail pincers,
the common European Earwig (*F. auricularia*)
was called by the Saxons *earwicga,*
which is to say "ear-beetle" or "ear worm,"
so named because it was believed
(erroneously, but when has that mattered?) to burrow
into the ears of men, producing afflictions
equal even to the effects of gossip.

It is as hard, without special instruction,
to distinguish the Earwig from related species
as it is to distinguish one defendant at law
from all others. Like most defendants, too,
the Earwig, once exonerated in legal Latin,
remains forever guilty in the mother tongue.

Be careful what names you allow to adhere to you.
Avoid going to Law. Or, when all else fails,
dig into your leaf-mold deeper than confusion.

Miriam Waddington (1917–2004)

In a Corridor at Court

I keep my hunger in a hollow eye,
the raining moments feed it, hope
placates it and large windows stand
forbiddingly across the polished halls;
they trap all shivering air between two walls,

And offer eyes the texture of a feast
made from sheeted glass and sooty brick,
the dust motes hang in wheeling beams of sun
and unstained light lends clear austerity;
only my brow is weighed by iron bars

Which criss-cross window like a bloodied rope,
or press like law with all its heavy books
against lost freedom's lovely antelope
whose leap has left a mark upon the air,
and stirred the stillness in the corridor.

In the window lamps hang white and chaste,
they portion space and drag it infinite
beyond the brick into some larger minute,
and now my eyes enjoy imagined taste
of all trapped air and rainbow, of the leap.

It's all so recent; paste me in the air
that moves from wall to window touching glass,
let me be space or promise, make me lover,
with fierce caress unlock these darkened bars,
undo my tongue, dissolve the flinty stars.

Robert Lowell (1917–1977)

Law

Under one law,
or two,
to lie unsleeping,
still sleeping on the battlefield . . .

On Sunday mornings,
I used to foray
bass-plugging out of season on
the posted reservoirs.

Outside the law.
At every bend I saw
only the looping shore
of nature's monotonous backlash.

The same. The same.
Then once, in a flash,
fresh ground, though trodden,
a man-made landscape.

A Norman canal
shot through razored green lawns;
black reflecting water arched
little sky-hung bridges of unhewn stone—

outside the law:
black, gray, green and blue,
water, stone, grass and sky,
and each unique set stone!

Mona Van Duyn (1921–2004)

The Poet Reconciles Herself to Politicians

Politics is, as it were, the gizzard of society,
full of grit and gravel.—THOREAU

The sharp and the coarse
grind our life into law,
dealing by force
with the heart's monstrous maw.

Wormy riches, pride's weed,
the hot mash of sex,
power's cold chickenfeed,
earned by bloody head-pecks—

Since fineness can't chasten
the internal roister
that greed gobbled raw,
let stony clods hasten,
or our great only oyster
may stick in our craw.

Alan Dugan (1923–2003)

Defendant

Someone kicked him so he limped.
Someone hit him and his flinch
shriveled his spine. He crawled to court
in answer to an ad that read:
"Justice, to be done, demands
some practice on whoever comes
in any way bent to her hand."

Anthony Hecht (1923–2004)

Death the Judge

Here's Justice, blind as a bat,
(Blind, if you like, as Love)
And yet, because of that,
Supreme exemplar of

Unbiased inquiry,
Knowing ahead of time
That nobody is free
Of crime or would-be crime,

And in accordance (closed
To Fortitude, Repentance,
Compassion) has composed
His predetermined sentence,

And in his chambers sits
Below a funeral wreath
And grimaces and spits
And grins and picks his teeth.

A. R. Ammons (1926–2001)

Strip: 55

if I say I did it, did I do it or
did someone else do or say he did it

or did I imagine I did it or that
someone else did: or did someone

say he heard someone else say he did
it: I take the pieces of action where

I find them: judge them by the
curvatures of their unfoldings, by

the reasonableness of their scripture:
it matters importantly who something

happens to, I know you know, and
if something was done, it can mean

a lot if you or I did it: so don't
get me wrong: sometimes I did what

I say I did—if memory serves,
memory filtered through by invention

and displacement: responsibility
bears where it can be placed: so,

oh, yes, I stick with a sort of
reality: but let the writer go:

let reality come true if it can at
the center of his fictions: let his

dreams be as if histories: let what
went before come after: but I didn't

do it, I didn't do it, they cry,
sometimes until they gurgle in the

rope or splatter the blade—and
sometimes, what's more, they didn't

do it: mostly, they did: some that
did it laugh all the way home: it's

hard to distribute justice fairly:
injustice happens: money talks

James Wright (1927–1980)

At the Executed Murderer's Grave

(for J. L. D.)

Why should we do this? What good is it to us? Above all, how can we do such a thing? How can it possibly be done? —FREUD

1

My name is James A. Wright, and I was born
Twenty-five miles from this infected grave,
In Martins Ferry, Ohio, where one slave
To Hazel-Atlas Glass became my father.
He tried to teach me kindness. I return
Only in memory now, aloof, unhurried,
To dead Ohio, where I might lie buried,
Had I not run away before my time.
Ohio caught George Doty. Clean as lime,
His skull rots empty here. Dying's the best
Of all the arts men learn in a dead place.
I walked here once. I made my loud display,
Leaning for language on a dead man's voice.
Now sick of lies, I turn to face the past.
I add my easy grievance to the rest:

2

Doty, if I confess I do not love you,
Will you let me alone? I burn for my own lies.
The nights eletrocute my fugitive,
My mind. I run like the bewildered mad
At St. Clair Sanitarium, who lurk,
Arch and cunning, under the maple trees,
Pleased to be playing guilty after dark.

Staring to bed, they croon self-lullabies.
Doty, you make me sick. I am not dead.
I croon my tears at fifty cents per line.

3

Idiot, he demanded love from girls,
And murdered one. Also, he was a thief.
He left two women, and a ghost with child.
The hair, foul as a dog's upon his head,
Made such revolting Ohio animals
Fitter for vomit than a kind man's grief.
I waste no pity on the dead that stink,
And no love's lost between me and the crying
Drunks of Belaire, Ohio, where police
Kick at their kidneys till they die of drink.
Christ may restore them whole, for all of me.
Alive and dead, those giggling muckers who
Saddled my nightmares thirty years ago
Can do without my widely printed sighing
Over their pains with paid sincerity.
I do not pity the dead, I pity the dying.

4

I pity myself, because a man is dead.
If Belmont County killed him, what of me?
His victims never loved him. Why should we?
And yet, nobody had to kill him either.
It does no good to woo the grass, to veil
The quicklime hole of a man's defeat and shame.
Nature-lovers are gone. To hell with them.
I kick the clods away, and speak my name.

5

This grave's gash festers. Maybe it will heal,
When all are caught with what they had to do

In fear of love, when every man stands still
By the last sea,
And the princes of the sea come down
To lay away their robes, to judge the earth
And its dead, and we dead stand undefended everywhere,
And my bodies—father and child and unskilled criminal—
Ridiculously kneel to bare my scars,
My sneaking crimes, to God's unpitying stars.

6

Staring politely, they will not mark my face
From any murderer's, buried in this place.
Why should they? We are nothing but a man.

7

Doty, the rapist and the murderer,
Sleeps in a ditch of fire, and cannot hear;
And where, in earth or hell's unholy peace,
Men's suicides will stop, God knows, not I.
Angels and pebbles mock me under trees.
Earth is a door I cannot even face.
Order be damned, I do not want to die,
Even to keep Belaire, Ohio, safe.
The hackles on my neck are fear, not grief.
(Open, dungeon! Open, roof of the ground!)
I hear the last sea in the Ohio grass,
Heaving a tide of gray disastrousness.
Wrinkles of winter ditch the rotted face
Of Doty, killer, imbecile, and thief:
Dirt of my flesh, defeated, underground.

W. S. Merwin (1927–)

Tool

If it's invented it will be used

maybe not for some time

then all at once
a hammer rises from under a lid
and shakes off its cold family

its one truth is stirring in its head
order order saying

and a surprised nail leaps
into darkness
that a moment before had been nothing

waiting
for the law

John Ashbery (1927–)

Ignorance of the Law Is No Excuse

We were warned about spiders, and the occasional famine.
We drove downtown to see our neighbors. None of them were home.
We nestled in yards the municipality had created,
reminisced about other, different places—
but were they? Hadn't we known it all before?

In vineyards where the bee's hymn drowns the monotony,
we slept for peace, joining in the great run.
He came up to me.
It was all as it had been,
except for the weight of the present,
that scuttled the pact we made with heaven.
In truth there was no cause for rejoicing,
nor need to turn around, either.
We were lost just by standing,
listening to the hum of wires overhead.

We mourned that meritocracy which, wildly vibrant,
had kept food on the table and milk in the glass.
In skid-row, slapdash style
we walked back to the original rock crystal he had become,
all concern, all fears for us.
We went down gently
to the bottom-most step. There you can grieve and breathe,
rinse your possessions in the chilly spring.
Only beware the bears and wolves that frequent it
and the shadow that comes when you expect dawn.

Philip Levine (1928–)

Possession

They thought they could go back
to find the same marked squirrels
nesting in the walnut trees
and that there would be some work
to do, something useful
and hard, and that they might please

their own need to be doing.
You know what they found. They found
themselves standing in your yard
awed by the gladiolus
and the absence of something
they knew. This had been free land,

they said, but now it was yours
who went in to call the law.

John Hollander (1929–)

Tailor-Made

How can a punishment fit a crime?
What's not ill-suited to a wrong?
The pants will always be too long;
Sisyphus got his overtime,
But how irrelevant! Being light
In a heavy, dark, and wrenching wind
Didn't drape well across the kind
Of shape poor dear Francesca's tight
Little hot games with Paolo took.
Sagging, with their braces frayed,
The overkill, the underplayed
Will always have an ugly look.

Thom Gunn (1929–2004)

Legal Reform

Condemned to life, a happier condemnation
Than I deserved, I serve my sentence full,
Clasping it to me at each indication
That this time love is not the paradox
By which, whatever it contains, my cell
Contains the absolute, because it locks.

It all led up to this, a simple law
Passed by ourselves, which holds me in its power.
Not till I stopped the theft of all I saw
Just for the having's sake, could it be passed.
Now I refer disposal of each hour
To this, a steady precedent at last.

My sentence stipulated exercise
Painful and lonely in the walks of death
With twittering clouds of spirits; still there lies
Beneath the common talk my single hope:
I must get back inside the cage of breath
For absence twitches on the loosened rope.

Marched off to happiness, I quarry stone
Hour after hour, and sweat my past away.
Already I have made, working alone,
Notable excavations, and the guard,
Turning desire, who eyes me all the day,
Has no use for his whip, I work so hard.

Condemned to hope, to happiness, to life,
Condemned to shift in your enclosing eyes,

I soon correct those former notions rife
Among the innocent, or fetter-maimed.
For law is in our hands, I realize:
The sentence is, condemned to be condemned.

X. J. Kennedy (1929–)

Police Court Saturday Morning

Hauled from their bunks in separate cells,
  The couples, bleary-eyed, in shock,
Enter a room where time stands still,
  Snipped by a brisk electric clock.

The drunks who last night beat their wives,
  The wives who tried to carve their mates
By cops disarmed of kitchen knives,
  Disheveled, face the magistrate's

Hard glare and sit without retort,
  Snuggled in solitudes, bereft
Of will to save themselves. Love's short
  And when it's gone what else is left.

Charles Wright (1935–)

What I Am Trying to Say

What I am trying to say
Is this—I tell you, only, the thing
That I have come to believe:

Indenture yourself to the land;
Imagine you touch its raw edges
In all weather, time and again;

Imagine its colors; try
to imitate, day by day,
The morning's growth and the dusk,

The movement of all their creatures;
Surrender yourself, and be glad;
This is the law that endures.

Charles Simic (1938–)

At the Night Court

You've combed yourself carefully,
Your Honor, with a small fine-tooth comb
You then cleverly concealed
Before making your entrance
In the splendor of your black robes.

The comb tucked inside a handkerchief
Scented with the extract of dead roses—
While you took your high seat
Sternly eyeing each of the accused
In the hush of the empty courtroom.

The dark curly hairs in the comb
Did not come from your graying head.
One of the cleaning women used it on herself
While you dozed off in your chambers
Half undressed because of the heat.

The black comb in the pocket over the heart,
You feel it tremble just as ours do
When they ready themselves to make music
Lacking only the paper you're signing,
By the looks of it, with eyes closed.

Stephen Dunn (1939–)

Criminal

Born wrong. Could be as simple as that. Wrong parents. Wrong country. Or born anywhere, eminently decent, but on the wrong side of a bad law. Then there's the luck that separates forgotten incident from criminal one, like the time I accidentally set the corner lot ablaze, a nasty wind that day, no witnesses. I think too of the children I might have killed had they timed their carelessness just right, a trace of liquor on my breath, their ball rolling into the street, my car going slightly faster than slow. Fingerprinted. Front-paged. Instead, a normal evening at home, a citizen, nearly upright. Aren't most of us, caught or not, responsible for some kind of choice? And of course certain criminals calculate, plan, hide in the bushes, alter the books. So little separates me from them. Send us off into the wilderness without a goat, bearing our own burdens. Or maybe we deserve worse, or just to be left alone? We probably have more than one destiny, but one of them for sure is to meet up with ourselves, no Lord, no one to condemn or forgive.

Stephen Dunn (1939–)

Outlaw

A word with romance behind it; if he thinks of himself so named he can almost believe he's not a thug. He rides into town unnoticed, in a car these days. The law is the instrument of restriction he's habituated himself to disturb. As he sees it, the law would have a bull stop at red. It would reward the safe, those who wait—even when nothing's coming—for the light to change. The outlaw likes to elevate himself like this. He imagines songs sung about him, years after his death. Who alive, he thinks, is more alert than an outlaw? Who better knows where he is and what it takes to live another day? His definition of crime: a poor person's way of entering into his own rights. But he's only seen half the movie, remembered only the get-aways and the easy girls. He's the mistake he will make, which is why he can't see it. We would cry out and warn him, but our roles in the ancient dramas are fixed too.

Stephen Dunn (1939–)

History

It's like this, the king marries
a commoner, and the populace cheers.
She doesn't even know how to curtsy,
but he loves her manners in bed.
Why doesn't the king do what his father did,
the king's mother wonders—
those peasant girls brought in
through that secret entrance, that's how
a kingdom works best. But marriage!
The king's mother won't come out
of her room, and a strange democracy
radiates throughout the land,
which causes widespread dreaming,
a general hopefulness. This is,
of course, how people get hurt,
how history gets its ziggy shape.
The king locks his wife in the tower
because she's begun to ride
her horse far into the woods.
How unqueenly to come back
to the castle like that,
so sweaty and flushed. The only answer,
his mother decides, is stricter rules—
no whispering in the corridors,
no gaiety in the fields.
The king announces his wife is very tired
and has decided to lie down,
and issues an edict that all things yours
are once again his.
This is the kind of law
history loves, which contains

its own demise. The villagers conspire
for years, waiting for the right time,
which never arrives. There's only
that one person, not exactly brave,
but too unhappy to be reasonable,
who crosses the moat, scales the walls.

Ted Kooser (1939–)

The Witness

The divorce judge has asked for a witness,
and you wait at the back of the courtroom
as still as a flag on its stand, your best dress
falling in smooth, even folds that begin now
to gather the dust of white bouquets
which like a veil of lace is lifting
away from the kiss of the sunlit windows.

In your lap, where you left them, your hands
lie fallen apart like the rinds of a fruit.
Whatever they cupped has been eaten away.
Beyond you, across a lake of light
where years have sunk and settled to the floor,
the voices drone on with the hollow sound
of boats rubbing a dock that they're tied to.

You know what to say when they call you.

Seamus Heaney (1939–)

Punishment

I can feel the tug
of the halter at the nape
of her neck, the wind
on her naked front.

It blows her nipples
to amber beads,
it shakes the frail rigging
of her ribs.

I can see her drowned
body in the bog,
the weighing stone,
the floating rods and boughs.

Under which at first
she was a barked sapling
that is dug up
oak-bone, brain-firkin:

her shaved head
like a stubble of black corn,
her blindfold a soiled bandage,
her noose a ring

to store
the memories of love.
Little adulteress,
before they punished you

you were flaxen-haired,
undernourished, and your
tar-black face was beautiful.
My poor scapegoat,

I almost love you
but would have cast, I know,
the stones of silence.
I am the artful voyeur

of your brain's exposed
and darkened combs,
your muscles' webbing
and all your numbered bones:

I who have stood dumb
when your betraying sisters,
cauled in tar,
wept by the railings,

who would connive
in civilized outrage
yet understand the exact
and tribal, intimate revenge.

Seamus Heaney (1939–)

The Stone Verdict

When he stands in the judgment place
With his stick in his hand and the broad hat
Still on his head, maimed by self-doubt
And an old disdain of sweet talk and excuses,
It will be no justice if the sentence is blabbed out.
He will expect more than words in the ultimate court
He relied on through a lifetime's speechlessness.

Let it be like the judgment of Hermes,
God of the stone heap, where the stones were verdicts
Cast solidly at his feet, piling up around him
Until he stood waist deep in the cairn
Of his apotheosis: maybe a gate-pillar
Or a tumbled wallstead where hogweed earths the silence
Somebody will break at last to say, "Here
His spirit lingers," and will have said too much.

David Solway (1941–)

Wittgenstein at Chess

> And in this case it is so, not because the person to whom we give the explanation already knows rules, but because in another sense he is already master of a game.
> —PHILOSOPHICAL INVESTIGATIONS, 31

1. The rules by which we play
are only the conditions
of the game we happen to be playing.

2. They are not laws or immutable decrees
but necessary accidents,
evolutionary afterthoughts,
bones that tenon our parquetry.

3. The king, for example,
campaigning in the Orkneys
of his extravagance,
boasting of coastal sway and scope,
is the only piece that can be checked.

4. This was not given in Plato's handbook
of the eternal Form of chess
spelled out in *topos ouranios*
but happened somewhere along the way,
say, between India and Cambridge.

5. We are apprentices of the ludicrous.
The game precedes the rules
as we feint and thrust
along the lines
of a prior immeasurable quadratic

determining the set of our precisions,
specialists of the general.

6. Thus I decide to play
scholarly and frivolous as Hamlet
consulting the Tarot
on a Sunday afternoon
over tea and scones
in my rooms above the Quad;
or, as it may be, to speculate
on Manichaean doubles
in the locus of illusion,
the kingdom of warring particulars
squared in celluloid;
or to set an army of thoughts
marching down the page
towards ruin and imperial concessions.

7. But now I move this pawn
to block your clever theoretical bishop
and lock him into innocuous stasis
as the current of intrigue moves elsewhere
across the board that frames
our choices and encounters.

8. As for the rules, let us say
they consecrate
the freedom of the pieces
as they do our Seleucid flourishes
in the intricate roil of desire,
the first tactical gestures,
risk and probe of language
crowned by the syntax of consummation
as it happens to develop
between late afternoon and dusk.

9. And this is like chess
and not like chess,
and chess is also not like chess
but like that other game
whose borders defy the surveyor
in the realm where the rules merely ransom
our dark affinities and compulsions.

Robert Hass (1941–)

The Woods in New Jersey

Where there was only grey, and brownish grey,
And greyish brown against the white
Of fallen snow at twilight in the winter woods,

Now an uncanny flamelike thing, black
and sulphur-yellow, as if it were dreamed by Audubon,
Is turned upside down in a delicate cascade

Of new green leaves, feeding on whatever mites
Or small white spiders haunt underleafs at stem end.
A magnolia warbler, to give the thing a name.

The other name we give this overmuch of appetite
And beauty unconscious of itself is life.
And that that kept the mind becalmed all winter?—

The more austere and abstract rhythm of the trunks,
Vertical music the cold makes visible.
That holds the whole thing up and gives it form,

or strength—call that the law. It's made,
whatever we like to think, more of interests
than of reasons, trees reaching each their own way

for the light, to make the sort of order that there is.
And what of those deer threading through the woods
In a late snowfall and silent as the snow?

Look: they move among the winter trees, so much
the color of the trees, they hardly seem to move.

for Justice William J. Brennan, Jr.

William Matthews (1942–1997)

Negligence

A woman opens a parcel with no
return address. Last month her only son
drove himself full tilt into a maple
and each day brings new drudgery from grief.
What's this? A vase, an urn? Off with its lid.
And so she's up to her wrists in her son's
Ashes—not, by the way, like silt or dust,
but nubble and grit, boneshards and half-burnt
burls of cartilage, cinders and nuggets.
I ask you, ladies and gentlemen
of the jury, to glove her hands with yours
and sieve the rubble of your beloved
only son, and also I ask you this:
what simple task could the funeral home
perform to run this cruel film backwards,
to lift this woman's hands from the cinders
of her son and wind them back to her slack
lap, and why did these merchants of balm
fail to perform it? I believe you know
as well as I that it takes but paltry
seconds more to write a return address
than to endorse a check. It's easy to say
what they ought to have done, and did not do.
What's hard to know is how to value grief.
It's very hard—but it's the very job
you're here to do. You have to ask and ask,
Could this grief have been prevented? until you
answer. Money may seem a crude measure
in philosophy, though it seems exact
enough for the grocer's and mortician's

bills.
I beg your pardon, Your Honor.
I meant but to say that a jury's duty
is to blame or not to blame,
and if there's
fault there's got to be a reason for it,
and so a price for reason. What's honor
worth that's ladled like soup onto plates, all
the slosh that fits and then no more? Suppose
you pulled into a gas station and asked
for a full tank. "How far you gonna go?"
"Twelve miles east of Bozeman." "Then half a tank
will do." A freak mishap (golf course, four iron,
lightning) is one thing, and preventable
heartbreak another. This woman's bruised heart
is evidence, ladies and gentlemen
of the jury, and this plain brown paper
with no return address. If there's excuse
for every harm, what use then is law?
Ladies and gentlemen of the jury, I ask
you to vote against random pain, to vote
that suffering has cause and thus has blame,
to vote that our lives can be explained, and
to vote compensation for my client.

Paul Durcan (1944–)

This Week the Court Is Sleeping in Loughrea

The perplexed defendants stand upright in the dock
While round about their spiked and barred forecastle,
Like corpses of mutinous sailors strewn about the deck
Of a ghost schooner becalmed in summer heat,
Recline solicitors in suits and barristers in wigs and gowns,
Snoring in their sleeves.
On high, upon the judge's bench,
His Lordship also snores,
Dreaming of the good old days as a drunken devil
Dozing in Doneraile.
From a hook in the ceiling the Court Crier hangs,
His eyes dangling out of their sockets.
Below him the Registrar is smoothing the breasts of his spectacles.
In the varnished witness box crouches Reverend Father Perjury
With a knife through his back.
Behind him in the dark aisles, like coshed dummies, lurk
Policemen stupefied by *poitín.*
Up in the amphitheatre of the public gallery
An invisible mob are chewing the cud.
An open window lets in the thudding sounds of blows
As, on the green, tinker men brawl,
As they have done so there down the centuries—
The Sweeneys and the Maughans.
Such slender justice as may be said to subsist in Loughrea
Is to be discerned
In the form of a streamlet behind the house-backs of the town,
Which carries water out to the parched fields
Where cleg-ridden cattle wait thirsty in the shadowy lees,
Their domain far away from the sleeping courtroom of human battle.
Is it any surprise that there are children who would rather be cattle?

Eavan Boland (1944–)

The Hanging Judge

Come to the country where justice is seen to be done,
Done daily. Come to the country where
Sentence is passed by word of mouth and raw
Boys split like infinitives. Look, here
We hanged our son, our only son
And hang him still and still we call it law.

James Lynch Fitzstephen, magistrate,
First Citizen of Galway, 1493,
Spanish merchant trader, his horror
Of deceit a by-word, a pillar of society
With one weakness, Walter, whose every trait
Reversed his like a signature in a mirror.

The torches splutter, the dancing, supple,
Spanish-taught, starts. James Lynch Fitzstephen
May disapprove but he, a man of principle,
Recalls young Gomez is a guest in town,
And the girl beside, his son's choice, may restore
A new name and honour in an heir.

Dawn: Gomez dead, in a wood: the Spanish heart
Which softened to her rigid with the steel
Of Walter Lynch's blade. Wild justice there—
Now to its restraint, but not repeal,
he returns, friendless, to be met
By his father, mounted, hunting. In the stare

Which passed slowly between them, a history
Poises: repression and rebellion, the scaffold
And its songs, the principle unsung

Are clues in this judicial murder to a mystery
Unsolved still and only to be told
As a ghost story against a haunting.

As you, father, haunt me: the rope trails
From your fingers, below you the abyss.
Your arms balanced as the scales of justice,
You loop him while from your eyes fall other scales
Too late, tears of doubt, tears of remorse
Dropping on your own neck like a noose.

Thomas Lux (1946–)

Traveling Exhibit of Torture Instruments

What man has done to woman and man
and the tools he built to do it with
is pure genius in its pain. A chair of nails
would not do without a headrest of spikes
and wrist straps pierced with pins.
The Head Crusher, for example—"Experts disagree
about this piece: is it 17th or 18th century?"
This historical hatband contracts and contracts,
by screw, and was wrought by hand.
These skills, this craft, get passed along.
Take *The Red Hot Pincers and Tongs.*
They were "addressed mostly to noses, fingers, toes.
Tubular pincers, like the splendid crocodile
shown here, served to rip off . . ." I have been in pain
at museums, openings, but not
like this: *The Heretic's Fork*—"Placed
as it is, allows the victim only to murmur: I recant."
In all the pictures
the men and women chosen do not
appear in pain: sawed lengthwise,
wrecked on a rack or wheel, they do not
look in pain. And the torturers
(the business always official)
seem uninterested, often flipping
pages of a book—one of laws, of God.
It seems most times men did this or that,
so terrible to him or her,
it was because God willed it so.
Or, at least, they thought He did.

Yusef Komunyakaa (1947–)

Light on the Subject

Hello, Mister Jack
The Ripper, come on in
make yourself at home.
Here in Deadwood City
your hands are clean as ours.
Our eyes flash back to
knives on silver whetstones.
Can I get you anything, partner?
Perhaps a shot of Four Roses?
In this gray station of wood
our hearts are wet rags
& we turn to ourselves,
holding our own hands
as the scaffolds sway.
I can tell you this much
Brother Justice, our faith's
unshakable, even if we rock stones
asleep in broken arms.
We've all seen moonlight on lakes
& crows whittled from a block
of air. In this animal-night, no
siree, we won't disappoint you
when we rise out of hawkweed,
because we still have
a thing about Law
& Order.

Lawrence Joseph (1948–)

Admissions against Interest

I

Taking my time, literal as I seemed, crazy
enough for silly disputes, actually Asiatically

sorry-eyed, reconciled finally
to the fact the January snow

behind the silver shed was only that,
the sudden sense you've seen it all before

appearing to take shape. For the likes of me
the weather wasn't any theory,

only conflagrations of the specks of a scene,
of rain the smell of smoldering soot,

clouds sweeping crimson down the street,
a physical thing. Bound by the Continual

Ministries of Thine Anger—a funny sight,
on both knees, all or nothing

outside in, wanting evil to disappear,
a complex character rattling off his complexity

the way, in Arabic, my grandmother would.
Mind you, though, my primary rule:

never use the word "I" unless you have to,
but sell it cheaply to survive.

II

Now, what type of animal asks after facts?
—so I'm a lawyer. Maybe charming,

direct yet as circumspect as any other lawyer
going on about concrete forces of civil

society substantially beyond anyone's grasp
and about money. Things like "you too

may be silenced the way powerful
corporations silence, contractually"

attract my attention. The issue's
bifurcated. "Why divide the dead?"

the Foreign Minister asks, "what's one life
when you've lost twenty million?"

And if what has happened during my life
had been otherwise could I say

I would have seen it much differently?
Authority? Out of deeper strata

illuminations. A lot of substance
chooses you. And it's no one's business

judging the secrets each of us needs:
I don't know what I'd do without my Double.

III

So the times demanded figuring out,
and on winter evenings beams of violet

appeared, thin and violent. Gorgeous violet
avenue, gentle, frightened look. The state's agency

assigned to the task of measuring toxicological
effects on the sticky matter

of recollection cells doesn't have any idea.
The air roundabout the Bridge can't be

gold. "You know it makes you want to
shout," the girl on the bus, laughing, shouts,

throws both her hands up, the same song
tuned up on her radio, and I'm off into a mood again,

another internal swoon. So certain combinations
never before are worked on and hard,

knowing early on I could never act
as if I didn't think. My best cogitations

dwell in air so thick it weighs
on the skin, a solid complex, constrained

by this woman's clear fierce eyes wet
in this rain either with rain or with tears.

IV

And so I've had, vast and gray, the sky
my heart, amazed, determined by

the sight of a shimmering simulacrum,
undisturbed color. My admissions

against interest look smaller,
confirmations of another order.

My ancestors are on another plane,
never wholly innocent feeling any horror,

soul-contracted children of common cells,
never wholly distributed sensations

dejected into vertical visions and desire.
So l too am late at my singing,

too much to the point, but now I'm seeing
words are talk and words themselves

forms of feeling, rose-colored splashings
the ice-cold dawn, reliance upon

bare winds pouncing that dot of fire
inside compressed half-luminous air

deflected out of those places I see
formed into feeling, patches of light.

Rita Dove (1952–)

Twelve Chairs

My logic was not in error, but I was.

FIRST JUROR

Proof casts a shadow;
doubt is to walk
onto a field
at high noon
one tendril
held to
the
wind.

SECOND JUROR

A stone to throw

A curse to hurl

A silence to break

A page to write

A day to live

A blank

To fill

THIRD JUROR

between the lip
and the kiss
between the hand
and the fist
between rumor
and prayer
between dungeon
and tower
between fear
and liberty
always
between

FOURTH JUROR

Cancel the afternoon
evenings mornings all
the days to come
until the fires
fall to ash
the fog clears
and we can see
where we
really
stand.

FIFTH JUROR

How long will
this take?
I am not my
brother,
thank you;
my hands are
full already
taking care
of
myself.

SIXTH JUROR

I'm not anyone more
than anyone else.
I did my job, then
looked into
their eyes.
What had I
become?

SEVENTH JUROR

In the mind of the crow
burns a golden cry In
the heart of the mole
an endless sky In
the eye of the trout
shines a galaxy
And I who see this
tell no one
I who am
a corridor
longing
to be
field

EIGHTH JUROR

Look around:
magic everywhere.
Behind you,
tears and shadow.
Ahead the path
clean flame.
Look up, the air
is singing:
Underfoot
your shadow
waits.

NINTH JUROR

Not the eyes—never
look into the eyes.
The soul either
strikes out
or
trembles
beneath
the blow.

TENTH JUROR

Tragedy
involves
one.
History
involves many
toppling
one
after
another.

ELEVENTH JUROR

You can't mop the floor
before the milk's
been spilled;
you can't run off
if your shadow
is pinned
to
the wall.

TWELFTH JUROR

why is the rose
how is the sun
where is first
when is last
who will
love us
what
will
save
us

THE ALTERNATE

—And who are you?
—Nobody.
—What do you do?
—I am alive.
—But who'll vouch
for you?
—Listen closely,
you'll hear
the
wind.

Brad Leithauser (1953–)

Law Clerk, 1979

My fingers having checked and re-checked my tie,
I'm at ease—or nearly so. We're lunching high
over Manhattan, a hundred floors above
streets new to me still. He asks whether I

find the work "exciting." Behind him a buffet
tastefully boasting shrimp, squid salad, paté,
beef, chicken, cheeses, and some good marinated
mushrooms, calls me to come boyishly away

and fill my plate a second time. And I'd love
another beer. I think he thinks that one's enough.
"Exciting? Very"—which is not untrue.
"Best of all"—I'm speaking off the (starchy) cuff—

"I liked the document search in Tennessee."
Indeed, I did. How strange, how fine to be
a someone someone flies a thousand miles
to analyze ancient business files! Now he—

but who is he? A *partner*, first of all,
by which is meant no confederate or pal
of mine, but a star in the firm's firmament.
He's kind, though, funny, and lunch is going well

enough—the conversation light, the view vast
beyond my farthest hopes. The kid's arrived at last:
not just New York, but New York at the top.
Just think of all the noontime views that passed

into the void because I wasn't here! Think
of the elevated wines I never drank
in this very room! The tortes I failed to eat!
—Lunch here is money in the memory bank.

Why, then, wishing I were somewhere else? Why
does my glance drift sidelongingly, my mind stray
from his fatherly banter? When will I shake
this shakiness? It's worse at night. I sometimes stay

late at the office. The place starts thinning out
by six; cleaning women, outfitted to fight
their bosses' daily disarray, marshal vacuums,
trashbins, brooms. Their leaving leaves me free to write,

or to try, as the city underfoot
starts breathing visibly, bubbles of light,
hundreds and hundreds, a champagne glitter
promising love and—more—a distant, delicate

loveliness. *Here* is inspiration. Yet the clock
clicks; my mind does not. Could this be "writer's block,"
nothing but that ailment which, like tennis elbow,
raises its victim's status? Yet it's no joke,

this scooped-out feeling, a sense that language
will never span the gap within. The Brooklyn Bridge,
trafficking in cars and literary ghosts,
shimmers mockingly below. I can't budge

the block; thwarted, I inch instead toward parody,
Keats' "On the Grasshopper and Cricket" to be
wittily urbanized as "The Snowplow
and the Lawnmower"; I'll set "The poetry

of earth is never dead" upon its head.
And yet, though I have the title, and the thread
of a joke as a starter's cord, "Snowplow" will not
start: some mechanical failure under the hood.

In a later, hopeless project Shakespeare
writes in a fancy bar—"To beer or not to beer"
and "The Singapore Slings and Sombreros
cost an outrageous fortune." I'm going nowhere . . .

Most nights, the air's sticky. Too hot to jog,
I take myself out for a walk, like a dog,
once round the block. Inside, endlessly, my
electric fan rustles like a paper bag;

and armed with a borrowed book called *Parodies*,
I rifle my old English 10 anthologies
in search of targets. It seemed this would be simple
but it's not. And I'm hot. And the nights pass

slowly. Then: a new month: still stuck, parodies lost,
when, wolfing lamb at lunch, I find I've crossed
Cinderella's fable (a cleaning woman swept
like me into moneyed worlds) with—Robert Frost.

"Whose shoe this is I need to know.
Throughout the countryside I'll go
In search of one whose gaze is clear,
Whose royal skin is white as snow."

Now *this* is simple, stanzas dropping into place,
and while I couldn't say precisely what it is
I'd like to say, just writing quickly is enough.
And the last stanza is, I think, quite nice:

"And if she's lost, I'll settle cheap—
A helpmate from the common heap,
Some kitchenmaid or chimneysweep,
Some kitchenmaid or chimneysweep."

What now?—next? Will the impasse pass? After work,
I'm roundabouting home through Central Park
when a voice cuts short all questions. "*Bradford.*"
It sounds like someone I hope it isn't. ". . . Mark."

He's wearing jeans and a work-shirt with a rip
in the neck, whereas I'm caught in the trap-
pings of a Wall Street lawyer. As we lob our
pleasantries across the Sartorial Gap

he studies me. Mark's a poet too, if you take
the thought for the deed—but who am I to talk?
At Harvard, hardly friends, we were nonetheless
drawn together by a fiercely sophomoric

contest: my-potential's-bigger-than-yours.
He's just in for the day, he quickly offers,
as if this were a kind of feat. City living
taints the artist's soul—he's suggesting of course—

which is his old, still tiresome refrain. So why
do I yet feel some need to justify
myself to him, who, he tells me, moved to a farm,
makes pots (a bad sign) and (I'm sure) lives high

on Daddy's bucks. His dad makes pots and pots
of money in securities—but let's
not hear me griping at the rich while wearing
one of my two two-hundred-dollar suits.

Mark draws from a knapsack the books he's bought—
Pound, Lawrence, Durrell (I thought he was out),
Smart and Clare (safer choices, both being mad)
and a surprising, handsome *Rubaiyat.*

Mark asks about my job. He has me twice
repeat my salary, each time bulging his eyes
in sham barefaced amazement. Later, alone
and gleefully free to wage my wars in peace,

I derail a quatrain (striking at that band
of Harvard potters who'd "live off the land"
a summer or two before going on
for M.B.A.'s, just as the parents planned):

"A Book of Verses underneath the Bough,
A Jug of Wine, a Loaf of Bread, and Thou—
sands in the Bank; fleeting though Riches be,
And powerless, They comfort anyhow."

Yes . . . And all at once, summer's nearly through.
I return *Parodies,* a week overdue.
And I'm asked to join the firm, beginning next year,
with four months to decide . . . Oftener now

I linger at work, to watch how the setting sun
at once sharpens and softens the skyline;
sometimes—the better for being rare—the dusk-light's
perfect and, while occupied toy boats twine

the Hudson with long, unraveling wakes,
the sun buffs hundreds of windows, reglazes bricks,
ruddies a plane's belly like a robin's,
and seems to free us from billable time, from stocks

and bonds (both words a pun, ironically,
on hand-fetters), leases, estate taxes, proxy
fights, adverse parties, complainants, claimants,
motions to suppress, to enjoin, to quash, oxy-

moronic lengthy briefs, and the whole courtly game
of claim and counterclaim; seems to say we come
through drudgery to glory . . . Look—down there! Wall
Street's turned to gold at last! And there are some

silver nights of emptied offices, raindrops
washing out the glue on those envelopes
in which memories are sealed and the entire
cleared distances offered up, all the old hopes

intact, as if nothing's been mislaid. This obscure
sense that one's past is safely banked somewhere
finds confirmation each time the recumbent
city, touched by darkness, begins to stir

and with a sufferance that's nearly heartbreaking
undergoes a pane by pane awakening
until just as fresh, as sparklingly replete
as last night, or any night before: *not a thing*

is lost. The frail headlights drift, as white as snow
it's fair to say. I'll leave here soon, for good. I know
"for good" is for the better, in some ways, and know
I'll be ready to leave. Or nearly so.

Martín Espada (1957–)

Mi Vida: Wings of Fright

The refugee's run
across the desert borderlands
carved wings of fright
into his forehead,
growing more crooked
with every eviction notice
in this waterfront city of the north.

He sat in the office for the poor,
daughter burrowed asleep
on one shoulder,
And spoke to the lawyer
with a voice trained obedient
in the darkness of church confessionals
and police barracks, Guatemalan dusk.

The lawyer nodded through papers,
glancing up only when the girl awoke
to spout white vomit on the floor
and her father's shirt.
Mi vida: My life, he said,
then said again, as he bundled her
to the toilet.
This was how the lawyer,
who, like the fortune-teller,
had a bookshelf of prophecy
but a cabinet empty of cures,
found himself
kneeling on the floor
with a paper towel.

Martín Espada (1957–)

The Legal Aid Lawyer Has an Epiphany

Chelsea, Massachusetts

When I bounced off the bus for work
at Legal Aid this morning,
I found the spiky halo of a hole
in the front window of the office,
as if some drunk had rammed
the thorn-crowned head of Jesus
through the glass.
I say Jesus because I followed
the red handprints on the brick
and there he was next door,
a bust in the window
of the botánica,
blood in his hair,
his eyes a bewildered blue
cast heavenward, hoping
for an airlift away from here.
The sign on the door
offered a manicure
with every palm reading.

Glyn Maxwell (1962–)

The Sentence

Lied to like a judge I stepped down.
My court cleared to the shrieks of the set free.
I know the truth, I know its level sound.
It didn't speak, or didn't speak to me.

The jury caught the tan of her bright look,
The ushers smoothed her path and bowed aside,
The lawyers watched her fingers as she took
Three solemn vows, her lipstick as she lied.

She vowed and lied to me and won her case.
I'm glad she won. I wouldn't have had her led
However gently into the shrunken space
I'd opened for her. There. There now it's said,

Said in this chamber where I sleep of old,
Alone with books and sprawling robes and scent.
With all I have, I have no power to hold
The innocent or the found innocent.

Seth Abramson (1976–)

If You Ask Your Attorney to Be Concise

When he speaks, it will not be to describe those neighbors you were born to,
whose boys like grim ferrets poked their heads out the weeds
and stole caps from your juiced Honda; because he knows you loved life
in the neighborhood / and may even have loved sending

your furtive retrievers, like warhorses, out to battle with the locals, and did
treat them well—your retrievers—once they'd plunged
down hillsides with red tongues and upturned noses, doing so only
because you'd asked them to, and sometimes meant it / he won't say

you believed in those dogs more than the three sons who were taken away,
though he knows you did, and knows it was because
they could better ride the downdraft of your discouragement, and had no fear
you would betray them / if not out of love

but because you, too, thrilled in the loose, uncertain spaces of the mudflats,
and thwarting a hardscrabble policeman, and were of course the one who
once, in a defile so bannered with vapor and sleet in grey hooks
even the mud spat back, fought one / and did so thanking your father,

your real father, for hitting you so hard, so often. So your man will say little
of a spindly wife who beetled her way through the valley leading off
and away from you, the intemperate years no more than a desultory jumble
in the back seat of her Duster / *good riddance*

is all you said to her, *good riddance.* And from this din there isn't any sound
your advocate will extract, not a single note he'll find to ride this chaos

home—not the snap of the infant you in a washer,
        or the teen you cradling an oily pistol / or the eternal synaptic you

who might find, in the thinning daylight ahead, that one ferocious moment
to live in forever, in which there is no love left
but the love of those moments which precede every moment of regret,
        obscure lullabies / with nothing to hang their words upon

but the bony grapples of your wrists, which your defender may briefly
   touch
as you turn to go—blank as a principle—into the stairwell
which leads you down to those men who, loveless but not disloyal, take
   odd
        pleasure / as so many do / in knowing they'll never see you again.

Notes on Poems and Poets

The following notes are not intended to be exhaustive but rather to illuminate law-related details of the poems and of the authors' biographies, while also providing glosses of archaic, foreign, and dialect terms.

GEOFFREY CHAUCER, from the general prologue to *The Canterbury Tales*. It is possible, if far from certain, that as a young man Chaucer studied law at the Inner Temple. We do know that he served as Justice of the Peace for Kent between 1385 and 1389 and that he held other government posts (as a diplomat, a member of Parliament, and a customs official) that required a substantial knowledge of the law.

As a "sergeant" (or serjeant), Chaucer's barrister occupies the top rung of the medieval legal profession. The small body of serjeants had a monopoly on pleading in the Common Bench, and it was from their ranks that judges were drawn.

Line 1, *war*: prudent; 2, *Parvys*: the porch of St. Paul's Cathedral in London, where serjeants customarily gathered; 6, *assise*: the court of assizes; 7, *patente*: letter of appointment from the king; 10, *purchasour*: purchaser (of land); 11, *fee simple*: the broadest property interest allowed by law; 12, *infect*: invalidated; 15, *termes*: law books; *caas and doomes:* cases and judgments; 17, *endite*: write; *make a thing*: draft a document; 18, *coude no wight pinche at*: no one could find a flaw in; 19, *plein*: recite; 20, *hoomly*: modestly; 21, *ceint*: belt; *barres*: stripes.

WILLIAM DUNBAR, "Tydingis fra the Sessioun." In fifteenth-century Scotland, the highest court of justice met three times a year in Edinburgh. Dunbar satirizes the workings of the session by putting the poem in the mouth of a naive countryman, shocked by the corruption he encounters.

Line 1, *murlandis*: rustic; *uplandis*: countrified; 3, *tydingis*: news; *peax or weir*: peace or war; 4, *rownit*: whispered; 6, *lichtit of my meir*: alighted from my mare; 13, *prevenis a futher*: forestalls a great number (of people); 17, *fa*: foe; *oxstar*: upper arm; 18, *patteris*: murmurs (prayers); *beidis*: (rosary) beads; 20, *beckis*: bows; 21, *luke*: look; 22, *bydand*: waited for; *layis land in wed*: mortgaging land; 23, *super expendit*: broke from overspending;

24, *menis*: influence; 26, *feid*: enmity; *flemis*: banish; 29, *summondis*: writs; *exceptis*: objects; 30, *skaild*: scattered; *keppis*: catches; 31, *tynis*: loses; 32, *wynis*: wine; 34, *herreit*: is reduced to poverty; *on creddens dynis*: dines out on credit; 37, *tod:* fox; 38, *tursis*: carries; 41, *sanis the Sait*: blesses the court; 44, *wow*: woo; 45, *Carmeleitis and Cordilleris*: two orders of friars; 46, *genner*: engender; 48, *leiris*: learns; 52, *hait*: hot; *dantis*: subdue; 53, *faderlyk*: fatherlike; *pechis*: labored breaths; 55, *eirandis*: requests.

EDMUND SPENSER, from *The Faerie Queene*. In 1568, Queen Mary I of Scotland (Mary, Queen of Scots), fleeing her political enemies, sought refuge in England. Elizabeth I, fearing Mary as a rival claimant to the English throne, ordered her held under house arrest. After nineteen years of imprisonment, Mary was charged with complicity in a plot to assassinate Elizabeth. Convicted of treason, she was beheaded in February 1587. In Spenser's allegory, "Duessa" stands for Mary and "Mercilla" for Elizabeth. "Blandamour" and "Paridell" are the earls of Northumberland and Arundel, who had taken part in a previous conspiracy against Elizabeth. "Zele" probably represents Lord Burleigh, who led the prosecution of Mary.

Stanza 2, *enured*: committed; 6, *fact*: deed; 7, *appose*: examine.

SIR WALTER RALEIGH, "The Passionate Man's Pilgrimage." In 1603, Raleigh was tried and convicted of treason for conspiring against King James I. After a long imprisonment in the Tower of London, he was beheaded in 1618.

Raleigh was convicted largely on the hearsay testimony, extracted under torture, of his friend Lord Cobham. Raleigh's passionate demand at trial—"I claim to have my accuser brought here face to face to speak"—is said to have influenced the development of the hearsay rule in common law and, eventually, the Confrontation Clause of the U.S. Constitution (quoted in George Fisher, *Evidence* [New York: Foundation Press, 2002], 335).

Line 5, *gage*: pledge; 25, *suckets*: confections; 42, *angels*: gold coins, as well as celestial beings.

WILLIAM SHAKESPEARE, Sonnet 35. Noting the great density of legal reference in his plays, some scholars suggest that Shakespeare may have worked as a law clerk before becoming a playwright. There is, however, no extrinsic evidence for this. Shakespeare would certainly have absorbed some legal knowledge through his associations with the aristocratic young law students of the Inns of Court. It is known that Shakespeare's company performed some of his plays in the large dining halls of the Inns, where theatrical performances were frequently staged. Henry Wriothesley, the Earl of Southampton—to whom Shakespeare dedicated *Venus and Adonis* and who may have been the beloved young man of the sonnets—studied at Gray's Inn.

Line 13, *accessary:* accessory.

WILLIAM SHAKESPEARE, Sonnet 49.

Line 11, *against my self uprear*: as if testifying to swear truthfully, against himself, in court.

WILLIAM SHAKESPEARE, Sonnet 134.

Line 7, *surety-like*: as one who pledges security for another's bond.

SIR JOHN DAVIES, "Into the Middle Temple of My Heart." Davies studied law in the Middle Temple before going on to a distinguished legal and political career. He served as both Solicitor General and Attorney General for Ireland and in 1626 was appointed Lord Chief Justice of the King's Bench (although he died before he could take up the post).

Line 9, *convented*: convened; 10, *bencher*: one of the group of senior barristers who governed the Inns of Court.

BEN JONSON, "An Epigram to the Counsellor." The name in brackets appears as a blank in the manuscript version of the poem, but Jonson presumably refers to Sir Anthony Benn, a distinguished barrister.

JOHN DONNE, Satire 2. Donne resided at Lincoln's Inn from 1592 to 1596. How seriously he took the study of law is a matter of debate. In later life he lamented that "an hydroptique immoderate desire of humane learning and languages" had distracted him from his legal studies (R. C. Bald, *John Donne: A Life* [Oxford: Oxford UP, 1970], 79). But Donne's first biographer, Izaak Walton, records that at Lincoln's Inn he "gave great testimonies of his wit, his learning, and his improvement in that profession," that is, law (Bald, *John Donne*, 58). At any rate, Donne was never called to the bar. But when the middle-aged poet, frustrated in his quest for high government office, took holy orders, one of his first posts in the church was as preacher to the benchers of Lincoln's Inn.

On the figure of "Coscus," see introduction. The parenthetical aside in lines 11–13 refers to the legal procedure that permitted a condemned prisoner to escape the gallows by pleading "benefit of clergy." The test of the defendant's literacy (and therefore clerical status) was his ability to translate a passage from the Bible—a so-called neck-verse.

Line 20, *pistolets*: pistols or Spanish coins; 37, *canonists*: canon (ecclesiastical) lawyers; 41, *pox*: syphilis; 50, *tricesimo of the queen*: the thirtieth year of Elizabeth I's reign (1588); 53, *Hillary term*: the court term extending from late January to early February; 54, *'size*: court session; 55, *remitter*: the principle by which someone having two titles to an estate is deemed to hold it by the earlier or more valid one; 59, *Sclavonians*: Dalmatians (famed for the supposed ugliness of their speech); 68, *suretyship*: liability for another's debt; 75, *Simony*: selling of church offices; 86, *pulling prime*: drawing a winning hand at cards; 88, *assurances*: pledges (of land); 94, *Pater nosters*: Our Fathers (referring to the prayer); 98, *ses heires*: (Law French) his heirs; 106, *Carthusian fasts*: fasts by an order of monks noted for their abstemiousness.

JOHN DONNE, Satire 5. This poem was presumably written while Donne served as secretary to Sir Thomas Egerton, Lord Keeper of the Great Seal. Egerton was engaged in an effort to root out corruption in the English courts, especially the Star Chamber. But when, in 1601, Donne eloped with Egerton's niece, the Lord Keeper's patronage of the poet came to an abrupt halt.

Line 27, *wittols*: complaisant cuckolds; 28, *empress*: Elizabeth I; 42, *Angelica*: a character in the Italian poet Ariosto's *Orlando Furioso*, who escapes from her enemies while they fight over her; 44, *fee*: bribe; 59, *angels*: gold coins; 65, *pursuivant*: officer employed to find and arrest disguised Roman Catholics; 85, *the great Carrick*: a huge Spanish merchant ship seized by the English; 86, *leese*: lose.

ROBERT HERRICK, "Upon Case." Herrick's poem is a free version of an epigram by the Roman poet Martial (1.97), mocking a lawyer for his timidity in court.

Line 5, *serjeant*: see note to Chaucer, from the general prologue.

EDWARD TAYLOR, Meditation 38. Taylor extrapolates on 1 John 2:1: "And if any man sin, we have an advocate with the Father, Jesus Christ the righteous."

Line 20, *registerer*: registrar; 21, *sergeants*: bailiffs; 36, *sub forma pauperis*: (Latin) in the form of a pauper, that is, as an indigent defendant.

DANIEL DEFOE, from "A Hymn to the Pillory." A fervent Dissenter, Defoe wrote a pamphlet that mocked the intolerance of the Church of England. Convicted of libel, he was sentenced to stand in a London pillory on three successive days.

Line 4, *The Shortest Way*: (the title of the offending pamphlet was *The Shortest Way with Dissenters*); 10, *knights of the post*: professional perjurers who frequented the courts, offering their testimony for a fee.

JONATHAN SWIFT, "The Answer to 'Paulus.'" Robert Lindsay, the author of the epigram on "Paulus," served as legal adviser to Swift in his capacity as dean of Saint Patrick's Cathedral, Dublin (and later was executor of the writer's will). The final line of the poem refers to the barrister Robert Marshall and the politicians William Connolly and Dick Tighe, each of whom was either a political or personal enemy of Swift's.

The satirical jabs at lawyers echo those delivered in part 4, chapter 5, of *Gulliver's Travels.*

"The Answer," line 42, *quanta patimur*: (Latin) How much we have to endure!; 80, *moidores*: Portuguese gold coins, current in England in Swift's time; 115, *lucus . . . a non lucendo*: (Latin) It is a grove by not being light. The point here is that things are sometimes described in terms of their opposite qualities, as the word *lucus* ([dark] grove) derives from *lucendo* (light) and a "council learned" is usually anything but.

ALEXANDER POPE, "Verbatim from Boileau." Published anonymously but attributed to Pope, this poem is, as the title indicates, a close translation of some lines by the French poet (and one-time lawyer) Nicolas Boileau. Pope substitutes "Westminster" for "Palais [de Justice]."

WILLIAM BLACKSTONE, "The Lawyer's Farewell to His Muse." On this poem, and Blackstone's biography, see introduction.

WILLIAM COWPER, "The Cause Won." As a young man, Cowper served an apprenticeship to a solicitor and then enrolled in the Middle Temple. Although he was called to the bar in 1754, he showed little commitment to the law and practiced only briefly.

ROBERT FERGUSSON, "The Rising of the Session." In the eighteenth century, the Court of Session was Scotland's supreme civil court (as it remains today). Fergusson satirically depicts the exodus of lawyers from Edinburgh at the end of a session.

Line 3, *finger-nebbs*: fingertips; 5, *lyart pow*: hoary head; 16, *siller*: silver; 17, *hain'd multer*: saved meal; 21, *ding*: drive; *dool*: care; 23, *dree*: endure; 24, *drouthy*: thirsty; 25, *ohon*: alas; 26, *dowie poortith*: sad poverty; *caldrife*: chilly; 27, *ablins*: perhaps; 29, *buick*: body; 31, *yap*: keen; 32, *barras*: enclosure; 38, *stoo*: nibble; *kebbuck*: cheese; *heel*: rind; 39, *eith*: easily; *gar*: make; *chiel*: child; 40, *unco vogie*: unusually happy; 42, *scart*: scrape; *cogie*: plate; 43, *dung*: stuck; 44, *lift*: sky; 45, *in tift*: upset; 47, *seenil*: seldom; 48, *stappit weym*: a full belly; 49, *gin*: if; 56, *Robin Gibb*: a tavern keeper; 57, *sib*: akin; 59, *daut*: pet; *Rib*: wife; 61, *vacance*: vacation; 63, *toom*: empty; 65, *soom*: swim; 72, *trock*: deal; 74, *your bickers whumble*: turn your cups upside down; 77, *joot*: liquor; 78, *weym*: belly; 80, *haf a reath*: a quarter year; 82, *prie*: taste; 83, *reaming graith*: frothing goods.

ROBERT BURNS, "Extempore in the Court of Session", was written to be sung to the tune of the song "Killie Crankie." In 1787, Burns attended the Court of Session in Edinburgh to observe the proceedings in a notorious divorce case. Here he contrasts the courtroom styles of the opposing counsel—Sir Ilay Campbell, the Lord Advocate, a distinguished lawyer but a stumbling speaker—and Henry Erskine, an orator of crushing eloquence.

Line 5, *tint*: lost; 6, *grapèd*: groped; 7, *fand*: found; 11, *awee*: a moment; 16, *linn*: waterfall.

GEORGE GORDON, LORD BYRON, from *Don Juan*. In these lines from Canto 10 of *Don Juan*, Byron implicitly contrasts two prominent Scottish barristers—his friend Francis Jeffrey (the "*you*" of the penultimate line) and his enemy Henry Brougham (whose name he puns on in the phrase "legal broom"). He suggests that thirty-nine out of forty lawyers resemble the corrupt Brougham rather than the upright Jeffrey.

PERCY BYSSHE SHELLEY, "To the Lord Chancellor." In 1814, Shelley left his wife Harriet for Mary Godwin. Two years later, Harriet committed suicide. In 1817, Harriet's father and sister brought a suit in the Court of Chancery, seeking custody of the couple's two children. Citing the poet's "highly immoral" conduct and principles (including his atheism and opposition to marriage as an institution), the Lord Chancellor, Lord Eldon, removed the children from Shelley's custody (Kenneth Neil Cameron, *Shelley: The Golden Years* [Cambridge: Harvard UP, 1974], 51). But Shelley prevailed in part when the guardianship went to a friend of Shelley's solicitor rather than to Harriet's family.

ROBERT BROWNING, from *The Ring and the Book.* In Rome in 1698, Count Guido Franceschini was tried, convicted, and executed for the murder of his wife—whom he had suspected of adultery—and her parents. Browning based his book-length poem *The Ring and the Book* on contemporary accounts of the trial. In these lines from Book 5, Guido addresses the court in an attempt to exonerate himself.

Line 22, *Ad judices meos*: (Latin) to my judges; 43, *Justinian's Pandects*: the Byzantine emperor's digest of ancient Roman law, which still served as the basis of law in the Rome of the late seventeenth century.

EMILY DICKINSON, "I Read My Sentence Steadily." Dickinson's life and works have intricate (and intimate) connections to the law. Her father, Edward Dickinson, was a prominent lawyer in Amherst, Massachusetts. A young attorney in her father's office, Benjamin Franklin Newton, became her first mentor in literature. It is probably Newton whom Dickinson had in mind when she wrote, "I had a friend, who taught me Immortality" (Alfred Habegger, *My Wars Are Laid Away in Books: The Life of Emily Dickinson* [New York: Random House, 2001], 218). In middle age, Dickinson developed an intense literary, and possibly romantic, relationship with Otis Phillips Lord, a judge on the Massachusetts Supreme Judicial Court.

EMILY DICKINSON, "I Had Some Things That I Called Mine." Dickinson's first editor, Mabel Loomis Todd, identified "Shaw" as "a man who used to dig for [Dickinson]—a day laborer" (R. W. Franklin, ed., *The Poems of Emily Dickinson: Variorum Edition* [Cambridge: Harvard UP, 1998], 139). More recent scholars have seen a humorous conflation of the workman with Lemuel Shaw, chief justice of the Massachusetts Supreme Judicial Court from 1830 to 1860.

LEWIS CARROLL, "The Barrister's Dream." Carroll's classic nonsense poem, *The Hunting of the Snark: An Agony, in Eight Fits*, first appeared in 1876. It tells the story of an oddly assorted crew (including a Bellman, a Bonnet Maker, and a Beaver) who go in search of an elusive creature called the Snark. Among the crew members is a Barrister, "brought to arrange their disputes." His "Dream" comprises "Fit the Sixth."

OSCAR WILDE, from *The Ballad of Reading Gaol*. In 1895, Wilde was convicted of gross indecency for having engaged in homosexual acts. He served two years at hard labor.

RUDYARD KIPLING, "The Reeds of Runnymede." At Runnymede in 1215, rebellious English barons forced King John I to sign the Magna Charta, thus securing their feudal liberties. The charter's guarantee of due process, paraphrased by Kipling in stanza 4, was interpreted by later generations of legal scholars as affirming the rights of habeas corpus and trial by jury.

EDGAR LEE MASTERS, "'Butch' Weldy," from *Spoon River Anthology*. Masters practiced law in Chicago for nearly thirty years, eight of them in partnership with Clarence Darrow, the most famous American lawyer of his time. His *Spoon River Anthology* consists of a cycle of 244 interlocking poems describing the life of a fictional Illinois village. Each poem takes the form of a dramatic monologue or spoken epitaph delivered by one of the residents of the Spoon River Cemetery.

The poems frequently reflect on legal issues or controversies. In "'Butch' Weldy," Masters displays the populist sympathies he shared with Darrow when he points to the harshness of the "fellow servant" doctrine (which prevented workers from recovering for injuries caused by fellow employees).

EDGAR LEE MASTERS, "Carl Hamblin," from *Spoon River Anthology*. In May 1886, a bomb exploded at a workers' rally in Haymarket Square, Chicago, killing seven policemen. Eight anarchist leaders (only one of whom had been present in the square) were subsequently indicted for murder, tried, and convicted. Masters was one of many observers who thought the proceedings fatally biased. Four of the anarchists were hanged in November 1887. Six years later, Governor Peter Altgeld, after concluding that all the defendants had been innocent, pardoned the surviving three (one having committed suicide).

WILLIAM CARLOS WILLIAMS, "Impromptu: The Suckers." In 1920, two Italian American anarchists, Nicola Sacco and Bartolomeo Vanzetti, were convicted of the murder of two men in the course of a payroll robbery in South Braintree, Massachusetts. The perception that the defendants were victims of political oppression and ethnic bigotry fueled protests across the globe. In 1927, after a series of failed appeals, Sacco and Vanzetti were sentenced to death. A special commission—appointed by the governor of Massachusetts and headed by A. Lawrence Lowell, president of Harvard—supported the jury's decision and recommended against clemency. Sacco and Vanzetti were electrocuted in August, 1927. Scholarly debate continues as to the question of their guilt.

D. H. LAWRENCE, "Auto-da-Fé." Long after Lawrence's death, his novel *Lady Chatterley's Lover* would be the subject of landmark obscenity trials in the U.S. (1959) and the U.K. (1960). In a lesser-known episode of 1929, an exhibition of Lawrence's paintings was raided by the London police, who confiscated thirteen of the works as obscene. In court, the eighty-two-year-old magistrate Frederick Meade ordered the gallery owner to show cause why the paintings should not be destroyed. Meade declared the question of artistic quality "utterly immaterial": "The most splendidly painted picture in the universe might be obscene" (Edward de Grazia, *Girls Lean Back Everywhere: The Law of Obscenity and the Assault on Genius* [New York: Random

House, 1992], 87). Ultimately, the government relinquished the pictures with the condition that they never again be exhibited in England.

EDNA ST. VINCENT MILLAY, "Justice Denied in Massachusetts." On August 22, 1927, the day before the scheduled executions of Sacco and Vanzetti (see note to Williams, "Impromptu: The Suckers"), Millay met with Massachusetts Governor Alvan T. Fuller to plead for clemency. The executions went ahead as scheduled.

CHARLES REZNIKOFF, from "Early History of a Writer." Reznikoff attended New York University Law School. Admitted to the bar in 1916, he practiced only briefly, preferring to devote himself to writing. Later, however, his work as an editor on the legal encyclopedia *Corpus Juris* would inspire his most ambitious literary project—*Testimony*, a two-volume cycle of poems representing the history of late nineteenth- and early twentieth-century America through the paraphrased facts of appellate cases.

Reznikoff was associated with the school of poetry known as Objectivism, which he defined as the theory that a poet should write only about "what he sees and hears," as if he were "restricted almost to the testimony of a witness in a court of law" (quoted in Benjamin Watson, "Reznikoff's Testimony," *Legal Studies Forum* 29, no. 1 [2005]: 69).

STEPHEN VINCENT BENÉT, from *John Brown's Body*. In 1859, the radical abolitionist John Brown led a group of his followers in occupying the federal arsenal in Harpers Ferry, Virginia (now West Virginia). A combined force of militiamen and federal troops quickly defeated the abolitionists. Brown was tried for treason, convicted, and hanged, becoming the antislavery movement's most important martyr.

YVOR WINTERS, "To Edwin V. McKenzie." In 1933, when Winters was a professor at Stanford University, a Stanford employee named David Lamson was charged with murdering his wife, who had been found dead in the bathtub. After a jury convicted Lamson of the murder, Winters and other members of the Stanford community who were convinced of his innocence helped organize his appeal. Lamson's appellate attorney, Edwin McKenzie, took his case to the California Supreme Court, which overturned Lamson's conviction. After three subsequent mistrials, the state dropped its case against Lamson.

LANGSTON HUGHES, "The Town of Scottsboro." In Alabama in 1931, nine young African American men were accused of raping two white women aboard a freight train. Tried by all-white juries in the town of Scottsboro, eight of the nine men were found guilty and sentenced to death. The following year, the U.S. Supreme Court reversed the convictions, holding (in *Powell v. Alabama*) that the defendants had been denied due process of law. During the second set of trials, one of the alleged victims recanted her original testimony, insisting that the assault had never occurred. Nevertheless, four of the nine "Scottsboro Boys" were again convicted of rape. Although all escaped execution, the last defendant was not released from prison until 1950.

ROY FULLER, "The Verdict." Like Wallace Stevens, the British writer Roy Fuller combined a distinguished poetic career with that of an in-house company lawyer. For three decades (with time out for service in World War II), Fuller worked as a solicitor for the Woolwich Building Society, a home-mortgage firm. In 1968, he was elected to the honorary post of Professor of Poetry at Oxford.

MURIEL RUKEYSER, "The Trial." See note to Hughes, "The Town of Scottsboro."

MIRIAM WADDINGTON, "In a Corridor at Court." Trained as a social worker, Waddington worked for a number of years in the courts and prisons of her native Canada.

JAMES WRIGHT, "At the Executed Murderer's Grave." In an interview, Wright discussed the genesis of this poem: "I was preoccupied with how, back in Ohio, a taxi driver from Belaire drove a girl out in the country and made a pass at her, which she resisted, so he banged her in the head with a tree branch and killed her. . . . I thought it was ridiculous to execute him and, further, I thought that murder is murder whether the state commits it or some stupid, retarded taxi driver" (Dave Smith, "James Wright: The Pure

Clear Word, an Interview," in *The Pure Clear Word: Essays on the Poetry of James Wright*, ed. Dave Smith [Urbana: U of Illinois P, 1982], 20).

PAUL DURCAN, "This Week the Court is Sleeping In Loughrea."
Line 17, *poitín*: Irish moonshine.

LAWRENCE JOSEPH, "Admissions against Interest." A graduate of the University of Michigan Law School, Joseph practiced at the firm of Shearman and Sterling before becoming a professor at St. John's University School of Law, where he teaches courses in torts, employment law, and jurisprudence, as well as law and literature. He has published five books of poems and the prose work *Lawyerland.*

RITA DOVE, "Twelve Chairs." In a note to this poem, Dove writes, "Most of these pieces—some in slightly different form—can be found carved on the backs of twelve marble chairs in the lobby of the Federal Court House in Sacramento, California, as part of an installation by designer Larry Kirkland" (Rita Dove, *American Smooth* [New York: Norton, 2004], 140).

BRAD LEITHAUSER, "Law Clerk, 1979." After graduating from Harvard Law School, Leithauser worked for three years as a research fellow at the Kyoto Comparative Law Center in Japan. The author of five books of poetry, five novels, and one novel in verse, he teaches in the writing seminars at Johns Hopkins University.

MARTÍN ESPADA, "Mi Vida" and "The Legal Aid Lawyer Has an Epiphany." A graduate of Northeastern University School of Law, Espada served for several years as a tenants' lawyer and supervisor of a legal services program. The author of nine collections of poetry, he teaches in the Department of English at the University of Massachusetts Amherst.

SETH ABRAMSON, "If You Ask Your Attorney to Be Concise." Abramson, who graduated from Harvard Law School, worked for six years as an attorney with the office of the New Hampshire Public Defender. He holds an M.F.A. from the Writers' Workshop at the University of Iowa. His first collection of poems, *The Suburban Ecstasies,* appeared in 2009.

Permissions

Seth Abramson, "If You Ask Your Attorney to Be Concise." From *The Suburban Ecstasies* by Seth Abramson. Copyright © 2009 by Seth Abramson. Reprinted by permission of the author and Ghost Road Press.

A. R. Ammons, "Strip: 55." From *Glare* by A. R. Ammons. Copyright © 1997 by A. R. Ammons. Used by permission of W. W. Norton and Company, Inc.

John Ashbery, "Ignorance of the Law Is No Excuse." From *Where Shall I Wander* by John Ashbery. Copyright © 2005 by John Ashbery. Reprinted by permission of HarperCollins Publishers.

W. H. Auden, "Law Like Love." From *Collected Poems* by W. H. Auden. Copyright © 1940, 1966, 1968 by W. H. Auden. Used by permission of Random House, Inc.

Stephen Vincent Benét, from *John Brown's Body* by Stephen Vincent Benét. Copyright ©1927, 1928 by Stephen Vincent Benét, renewed 1955 by Rosemary Carr Benét. Reprinted by permission of Brandt and Hochman Literary Agents, Inc.

John Berryman, "Dream Song 86." From *The Dream Songs* by John Berryman. Copyright © 1969 by John Berryman, renewed 1997 by Kate Donahue Berryman. Reprinted by permission of Farrar, Straus and Giroux, LLC.

Eavan Boland, "The Hanging Judge." From *An Origin Like Water, Collected Poems 1967–1987* by Eavan Boland. Copyright © 1975 by Eavan Boland. Used by permission of W. W. Norton and Company, Inc.

John Ciardi, "E Is for Earwig." From *An Alphabestiary* by John Ciardi. Reprinted by permission of Ciardi Family Publishing Trust.

J. V. Cunningham, "The Judge Is Fury." From *The Poems of J. V. Cunningham* by J. V. Cunningham, ed. Tim Steele. Copyright © 1997 by Swallow Press/Ohio University Press. Reprinted by permission of Swallow Press/Ohio University Press, Athens, Ohio (www.ohioswallow.com).

W. H. Davies, "The Inquest." From *Selected Poems of W. H. Davies* by W. H. Davies. Copyright © 1985 by Oxford University Press. Reprinted by permission of Oxford University Press.

Emily Dickinson, "I Had Some Things That I Called Mine," and "I Read My Sentence Steadily." From *The Poems of Emily Dickinson*, ed. Thomas H. Johnson. Copyright © 1951, 1955, 1979, 1983 by the President and Fellows of Harvard College. Reprinted by permission of Belknap Press of Harvard University Press and the trustees of Amherst College.

Rita Dove, "Twelve Chairs." From *American Smooth* by Rita Dove. Copyright © 2004 by Rita Dove. Used by permission of W. W. Norton and Company, Inc.

Alan Dugan, "Defendant." From *Poems Seven: New and Complete Poetry* by Alan Dugan. Copyright © 2001 by Alan Dugan. Reprinted with the permission of Seven Stories Press (www.sevenstories.com).

Stephen Dunn, "Outlaw," "Criminal." From *Riffs and Reciprocities: Prose Pairs* by Stephen Dunn. Copyright © 1998 by Stephen Dunn. Used by permission of W. W. Norton and Company, Inc.

Stephen Dunn, "History." Used by permission of the author.

Paul Durcan, "This Week the Court Is Sleeping in Loughrea." From *A Snail in My Prime*. Copyright © 1993 by Paul Durcan. Reproduced by permission of the author c/o Rogers, Coleridge and White Ltd., 20 Powis Mews, London W11 1JN.

William Empson, "Legal Fiction." Copyright © 1928 by William Empson. Reproduced with permission of Curtis Brown Group Ltd., London, on behalf of the Estate of William Empson.

Martín Espada, "The Legal Aid Lawyer Has an Epiphany," "Mi Vida: Wings of Fright." From *Alabanza* by Martín Espada. Copyright © 1993 by Martín Espada. Used by permission of W. W. Norton and Company, Inc.

Kenneth Fearing, "The People v. The People." From *Complete Poems* by Kenneth Fearing. Copyright © 1938 by Kenneth Fearing, 1966 by the Estate of Kenneth Fearing. Reprinted by the permission of Russell and Volkening as agents for the author.

Roy Fuller, "The Verdict." From *New and Collected Poems, 1934–1984* by Roy Fuller. Reprinted by permission of John Fuller.

Thom Gun, "Legal Reform." From *Collected Poems* by Thom Gunn. Copyright © 1994 by Thom Gunn. Reprinted by permission of Farrar, Straus and Giroux, LLC.

Robert Hass, "The Woods in New Jersey." From *Sun under Wood: New Po-*

ems by Robert Hass. Copyright © 1996 by Robert Hass. Reprinted by permission of Harper Collins Publisher, Ecco Press.

Seamus Heaney, "Punishment." From *Poems 1965–1975* by Seamus Heaney. Copyright © 1980 by Seamus Heaney. Reprinted by permission of Farrar, Straus and Giroux, LLC.

Seamus Heaney, "The Stone Verdict." From *New and Selected Poems 1966–1987* by Seamus Heaney. Used by permission of Faber and Faber Limited.

Anthony Hecht, "Death the Judge." From *Flight among the Tombs: Poems* by Anthony Hecht. Copyright © 1995, 1996 by Anthony E. Hecht. Used by permission of Alfred A. Knopf, a division of Random House, Inc.

John Hollander, "Tailor-Made." From *Picture Windows: Poems* by John Hollander. Copyright © 2003 by John Hollander. Used by permission of Alfred A. Knopf, a division of Random House, Inc.

A. E. Housman, "Oh Who Is That Young Sinner." From *The Poems of A. E. Housman* by A. E. Housman, ed. Archie Burnett. Reprinted by permission of Oxford University Press.

Langston Hughes, "The Town of Scottsboro." From *The Collected Poems of Langston Hughes* by Langston Hughes, ed. Arnold Rampersad with David Roessel. Copyright © 1994 by the Estate of Langston Hughes. Used by permission of Alfred A. Knopf, a division of Random House, Inc.

David Ignatow, "The Law Has Reasons." From *New and Collected Poems, 1970–1985* by David Ignatow. Copyright © 1986 by David Ignatow. Reprinted by permission of Wesleyan University Press.

Lawrence Joseph, "Admissions against Interest." From *Codes, Precepts, Biases, Taboos* by Lawrence Joseph. Copyright © 2005 by Lawrence Joseph. Reprinted by permission of Farrar, Straus and Giroux, LLC.

Weldon Kees, "After the Trial." From *The Collected Poems of Weldon Kees,* ed. Donald Justice. Copyright 1962, 1975 by the University of Nebraska Press, renewed 2003 by the University of Nebraska Press. Reprinted by permission of the University of Nebraska Press.

X. J. Kennedy, "Police Court Saturday Morning." From *The Lords of Misrule.* Copyright © 2002 by X. J. Kennedy. Reprinted with permission of the Johns Hopkins University Press.

Yusef Komunyakaa, "Light on the Subject." From *Neon Vernacular: New and Selected Poems* by Yusef Komunyakaa. Copyright © 1993 by Yusef Komunyakaa. Reprinted with permission by Wesleyan University Press.

Ted Kooser, "The Witness." From *Flying at Night: Poems 1965–1985* by Ted Kooser. Copyright © 2005. Reprinted by permission of the University of Pittsburgh Press.

D. H. Lawrence, "Auto-da-Fé." From *The Complete Poems of D. H. Lawrence* by D. H. Lawrence, ed. V. de Sola Pinto and F. W. Roberts. Copyright © 1964, 1971 by Angelo Ravagli and C. M. Weekley, executors of the Estate of Frieda Lawrence Ravagli. Used by permission of Viking Penguin, a division of Penguin Group (USA) Inc.

Brad Leithauser, "Law Clerk, 1979." From *Hundreds of Fireflies* by Brad Leithauser. Copyright © 1981 by Brad Leithauser. Used by permission of Alfred A. Knopf, a division of Random House, Inc.

Philip Levine, "Possession." From *Not This Pig.* Copyright © 1968 by Philip Levine. Reprinted with permission of Wesleyan University Press.

Robert Lowell, "Law." From *Collected Poems* by Robert Lowell. Copyright © 2003 by Harriett Lowell and Sheridan Lowell. Reprinted by permission of Farrar, Straus and Giroux, LLC.

Thomas Lux, "Traveling Exhibit of Torture Instruments." From *New and Selected Poems, 1975–1995* by Thomas Lux. Copyright © 1997 by Thomas Lux. Reprinted by permission of Houghton Mifflin Harcourt Publishing Company. All rights reserved.

William Matthews, "Negligence." From *Time and Money: New Poems by William Matthews.* Copyright © 1995 by William Matthews. Reprinted by permission of Houghton Mifflin Harcourt Publishing Company. All rights reserved.

Glyn Maxwell, "The Sentence." From *The Boys at Twilight: Poems 1990–1995* by Glyn Maxwell. Copyright © 1995, 2000 by Glyn Maxwell. Reprinted by permission of Houghton Mifflin Harcourt Publishing Company. All rights reserved.

W. S. Merwin, "Tool." From *Writings to an Unfinished Accompaniment* by W. S. Merwin. Copyright © 1973 by W. S. Merwin. Reprinted with permission of the Wylie Agency, Inc.

Edna St. Vincent Millay, "Justice Denied in Massachusetts." Copyright © 1928, 1955 by Edna St. Vincent Millay and Norma Millay Ellis. Reprinted by permission of Elizabeth Barnett, the Millay Society.

Charles Reznikoff. From "Early History of a Writer." From *The Poems of Charles Reznikoff: 1918–1975* by Charles Reznikoff, ed. Seamus Cooney.

Copyright © 2005 by the Estate of Charles Reznikoff. Reprinted by permission of Black Sparrow Books, an imprint of David R. Godine, Publisher, Inc.

Muriel Rukeyser, "The Trial." From *The Collected Poems of Muriel Rukeyser* by Muriel Rukeyser. Copyright © 1935 by Muriel Rukeyser. Reprinted by permission of International Creative Management, Inc.

Carl Sandburg, "The Lawyers Know Too Much." From *Smoke and Steel* by Carl Sandburg. Copyright © 1920 by Harcourt, Inc., renewed 1948 by Carl Sandburg. Reprinted by permission of Harcourt, Inc.

Charles Simic, "At the Night Court." From *Unending Blues* by Charles Simic. Copyright © 1986, 1985, 1984, 1983 by Charles Simic. Reprinted by permission of Houghton Mifflin Harcourt Publishing Company.

David Solway, "Wittgenstein at Chess." From *Chess Pieces* by David Solway. Reprinted by permission of McGill–Queen's University Press and the author.

Dylan Thomas, "The Hand That Signed the Paper." From *The Poems of Dylan Thomas* by Dylan Thomas. Copyright © 1939 by New Directions Publishing Corp. Reprinted by permission of New Directions Publishing Corp.

Mona Van Duyn, "The Poet Reconciles Herself to Politicians." From *Firefall* by Mona Van Duyn. Copyright © 1992 by Mona Van Duyn. Used by permission of Alfred A. Knopf, a division of Random House, Inc.

Miriam Waddington, "In a Corridor at Court." From *Collected Poems* by Miriam Waddington. Reprinted by permission of Jonathan and Marcus Waddington.

William Carlos Williams, "Impromptu: The Suckers." From *Collected Poems: 1909–1939,* vol. 1. Copyright ©1938 by New Directions Publishing Corp. Reprinted by permission of New Directions Publishing Corp.

Yvor Winters, "To Edwin V. McKenzie." From *The Collected Poems of Yvor Winters* by Yvor Winters. Reprinted with the permission of Swallow Press/Ohio University Press, Athens, Ohio (www.ohioswallow.com).

Charles Wright, "What I Am Trying to Say." From *Country Music: Selected Early Poems* by Charles Wright. Copyright © 1991 by Charles Wright. Reprinted by the permission of Wesleyan University Press.

James Wright, "At the Executed Murderer's Grave." From *Above the River: The Complete Poems* by James Wright. Copyright © 1990 by Anne Wright.

Index